TALES FROM THE
GEORGIA TECH
SIDELINE

A COLLECTION OF THE GREATEST
YELLOW JACKET STORIES EVER TOLD

KIM KING
WITH JACK WILKINSON

SPORTS
PUBLISHING

Sports Publishing books may be purchased in bulk at special discounts for sales promotion, corporate gifts, fund-raising, or educational purposes. Special editions can also be created to specifications. For details, contact the Special Sales Department, Sports Publishing, 307 West 36th Street, 11th Floor, New York, NY 10018 or sportspubbooks@skyhorsepublishing.com.

Sports Publishing® is a registered trademark of Skyhorse Publishing, Inc.®, a Delaware corporation.

Visit our website at www.sportspubbooks.com.

10 9 8 7 6 5 4 3 2

Library of Congress Cataloging-in-Publication Data is available on file.

Series design by Tom Lau
Cover photo credit Georgia Tech Sports Information

Print ISBN: 978-1-61321-705-4
Ebook ISBN: 978-1-61321-743-6

Printed in the United States of America

To my loving wife Gail, who has been by my side since my playing days at Georgia Tech

CONTENTS

ACKNOWLEDGMENTS

In Atlanta, Gale Williams was essential to the completion of this project. Thank you, Gale. Thanks to former Georgia Tech Sports Information Director Allison George and her staff for providing photographs and information with a smile.

Jack would like to express his love and gratitude to his wife, Janet Ward, and daughters Katharine and Alison for all their goodness all these years.

He's grateful for the invaluable assistance of Gail King and Mary Katherine Pearson in the writing and editing of this book.

Finally, Jack thanks Kim King, a fine and courageous man.

INTRODUCTION

I t's a room with a view, all right. A spectacular view,
and one of the great venues in all of college football.
It's also my very favorite place to watch, and cover,
a football game.

It's especially so on a crisp autumn evening, when
the ESPN cameras return to campus, and the Atlanta
skyline's aglow in the Thursday night sky above Bobby
Dodd Stadium and beneath a harvest moon.

And best of all, for a native New York City guy, you
can take the subway to the game. You can do this, of
course, for a Columbia game. Or Penn, even Temple,
too. But then, you make the call: Columbia-Cornell, or
Georgia Tech-Florida State? Or now, Tech-Miami?

Then, on your way from the MARTA station to the
stadium, you'll stroll down North Avenue and stop by
The Varsity for two chili dogs, onion rings and an F.O.
(frosted orange shake), just as folks did during the glory
days of Dodd. In Dodd they trusted, and feasted on
french fries, Coca-Colas and Clemson.

Walk another block, and there it is: Bobby Dodd
Stadium at Historic Grant Field, capacity now 55,000
and long the home of Georgia Tech football.

The oldest on-campus stadium in Division I-A, it's
also the repository of so much of the game's great past.

If Georgia plays between the hedges in Athens, Tech
plays between the pages. The history pages. Here in the
heart of one of our great American cities, smack dab
downtown in the Centennial Olympic city, beats the
heart of Georgia Tech football.

The original Heisman: John Heisman, won 102 games and a national championship while coaching at Georgia Tech from 1904–1919.

It's all here: a sense of college football's storied past, its turn-of-the-21st-century present and now, in the super-sized Atlantic Coast Conference, its mega-conference future. With Louisville replacing Maryland, the ACC stays at fourteen teams. A fifteenth, non-football member Notre Dame, plays five ACC games.

Georgia Tech is the home of the Heisman. The authentic Heisman: John Heisman, who coached at the Georgia Institute of Technology from 1904-1919 and won 102 games and a national championship, and for whom the most hallowed individual award in all of sports—the Heisman Trophy—is named.

On a parcel of campus land known as "The Flats," a 5,000-seat stadium built by Tech students opened in 1913 and was christened Grant Field. In 1916, Heisman—seeking revenge for a 22-0 baseball loss the previous year to tiny Cumberland College, which had used professional ringers from Nashville—oversaw Tech's 220-0 annihilation of Cumberland, the most lop-sided victory in college football history.

That night, as he was wont to do, Heisman likely sent out for ice cream for Woo, the family poodle, to cele-brate. The following year, his Yellow Jackets went 9-0 and won the first of Tech's four national championships.

The second title came 11 years later, midway through Bill Alexander's distinguished quarter-century coaching tenure. In 1928, Georgia Tech's Golden Tornado fin-ished 10-0 and co-national champions. But not until Tech's only trip to the Rose Bowl, and only because of Roy "Wrong Way" Riegels's misguided sense of direc-tion.

In one of the strangest plays in college football history, California's Roy Riegels made a famous wrong-way run to set up Georgia Tech's Rose Bowl-winning touchdown.

Scooping up a Tech fumble, the California center raced downfield, ignored a teammate who shouted, "Stop, Roy! You're running the wrong way!", then replied, "Get away from me! This is my touchdown!" and finally was tackled at the one-yard line. Cal's one-yard line. Tech scored on the next play and won 8-7.

A tradition was born. No, not misdirection plays. Tech's bowl success. The Jackets, long one of college football's elite bowl teams, were 21-11 in bowl games after last season's 52-10 Humanitarian Bowl humbling of

Tulsa. It was the seventh straight season in which Tech appeared in a bowl, and, at the time, gave the Jackets the best bowl winning percentage (.656) of any school. But then, Bobby Dodd was the undisputed *bowlmeister* on The Flats.

From 1951–56, back when new bowls didn't suddenly sprout like mushrooms or dandelions, Dodd directed Tech to six consecutive bowl victories. Thrice in the Sugar Bowl, once each in the Orange, Cotton and Gator. Dodd's 1952 team, his greatest, finished 12-0 after dominating Johnny Vaught's Ole Miss Rebels 24-7 in the Sugar Bowl to give Tech a share of its third national championship.

For 63 years, Georgia Tech was blessed with a pigskin Holy Trinity virtually unmatched in college football annals: Heisman, Alexander and Dodd, the only three coaches in those six-plus decades. If Dodd (165-64-8, including 9-4 in bowls) was the winningest coach on The Flats, followed by Alexander (134-95-15) and Heisman (102-29-7), it wasn't just how often Dodd won, but how. "The gentleman coach of college football," they called him. Furman Bisher, the late esteemed columnist for the *Atlanta Journal-Constitution*, recalls how often he heard coaches say, "Bobby Dodd was the best sideline coach I ever saw."

Dodd sat on the sideline in a folding chair at midfield, wearing a fedora and tie, often sunglasses later in his career, and he didn't so much coach a game as orchestrate it. He was a maestro—Bear Bryant called him the best game-day coach he ever faced—and his audience was Atlanta society; dressed in style, ensconced in choice seats in the West Stands, they knew Grant Field was the place to be, and be seen, in Atlanta in the '50s (when Dodd beat Georgia eight years running and reigned supreme) and early '60s. Georgia Tech was the only game in town.

An Atlanta kid named Kim King came of age then, became a Tech fan, then came to play for Bobby Dodd. He became Dodd's last quarterback and, the coach would admit, his very favorite quarterback. King was stunned, and crushed, as were all Tech fans, when Dodd suddenly retired after an Orange Bowl loss to Florida ended the 1966 season.

After employing just three coaching legends in 63 years, Tech is now on its ninth coach (Paul Johnson) since Dodd's departure. King knew them all: as Bud Carson's first quarterback in King's last season at Tech; as an ardently involved alumnus and board member of the Georgia Tech Athletic Association; and as the radio color commentator for this, his 31st season of calling Tech football.

King endured the '70s, when three coaches tried to duplicate the glory days of Dodd. He suffered through Bill Curry's dismal early years before Curry revived Tech's fortunes—only to leave for Alabama. King knew Bobby Ross' deep frustration in his first two falls on The Flats; he rejoiced with Ross and his top aides, George O'Leary and Ralph Friedgen, when Georgia Tech astonished all and won the 1990 UPI national championship.

There was the disastrous Bill Lewis era. O'Leary's return and the resurrection of Tech as a national power. The home of the Heisman has never produced a Heisman Trophy winner. Two Tech quarterbacks finished second in the voting: Billy Lothridge in 1963, when Kim King was a Tech freshman; and the great Joe Hamilton, who did everything but beat FSU and win the Heisman.

After working so many years with the legendary Al Ciraldo, King was in the Tech broadcast booth with Wes Durham that November afternoon in 1999 when Georgia eschewed a sure field goal and Jasper Sanks fumbled—or did he?—at the goal line and Chris Young recovered to force overtime. King cringed when Luke Manget's field goal attempt was blocked, rejoiced when holder George Godsey—realizing it was a third-down kick—recovered the ball, then roared when Manget made good on his second chance.

Tech, 51-48. Delirium. Friedgen fell to his knees on the Tech sideline as Manget's kick flew true. The offensive coordinator had to be helped to his feet. Thousands of Georgia Tech fans stormed the field. In his last home game, Hamilton bid Bobby Dodd Stadium adieu in grand style: victorious, and hoisted aloft by Tech students, then borne around the field.

Thirty-three years earlier, King got the royal treatment, too. After unbeaten and ninth-ranked Georgia Tech beat No. 8 Tennessee 6-3, King was borne on the shoulders of several Tech nerds—bespectacled freshmen who wore "Rat Caps" (the beanies mandatory for all freshmen) and carried King from Grant Field.

Now it's Bobby Dodd Stadium at Grant Field. For 50 years, Kim King had a view unlike any other. In my view, his view was unmatched. You'll see.

One

ONLY THE
BEGINNING

O n the morning of January 3, 2004, I woke up
in Boise, Idaho for, of all things, a bowl game.
In a few hours, Georgia Tech was going to play
Tulsa in the Humanitarian Bowl. It was still dark, freezing
cold, and it had snowed again overnight. It reminded me
of 1978, when Tech played at Air Force and Eddie Lee
Ivery set what was then the NCAA single-game rushing
record.

There were a lot of similarities that day in Boise: It was
overcast with gray skies. It was snowing, and the wind was
blowing. The conditions were just miserable.

Yet on that day, under those terrible conditions, both
there and back in Colorado Springs, I saw two of the most
remarkable rushing performances ever seen in college
football history: Eddie Lee's record-breaking, 356-yard
performance, and P.J. Daniels's great day against Tulsa.

I did the game on radio with Wes Durham in Boise, and had a flashback to that day at Air Force with Al Ciraldo.

BACK IN COLORADO

It was so cold that November day in Colorado Springs. The Tech fullback, Ray Friday, had backed into a commercial space heater on the sidelines that shot out a huge butane flame. He was so cold and numb later in the game, he tried to get warm by backing up toward the heater.

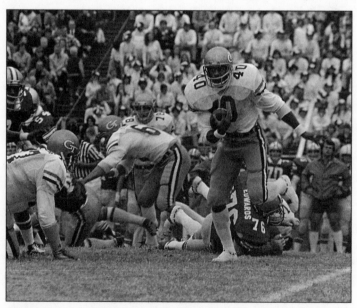

Eddie Lee Ivery (40) ignored the snow and the Air Force defense to rush for an NCAA single-game-record 356 yards in 1978.

All of a sudden, Ray was knocked down by a trainer or a manager. His pants were on fire. But he was just thinking about fighting the guy until someone explained he was just trying to help him.

For the rest of the game Ray had a big, black singed spot on the seat of his pants. Every time he got down in that fullback stance in the wishbone, squatting, it looked like he was mooning the crowd.

Even Ciraldo had to laugh. A manager was just trying to save Ray's, well, butt. And there was Ray, saluting the crowd, every play he was on offense. His blocking helped Eddie Lee rush for 356 yards and set the NCAA record.

REMINISCING

I've seen some really good places thanks to Georgia Tech football, and some really bad places. With all due respect to Boise and the Humanitarian Bowl, there was not much to see or do out there—except find a place to stay warm.

But I got to see the second best individual rushing performance in Georgia Tech history, and certainly one of the best in the 50 years I've been watching Tech football. P.J. Daniels rushed for 307 yards, the most in any bowl game, and he barely played in the fourth quarter.

He had 254 yards in the first three quarters, then got 38 more on his first carry of the fourth. P.J. could've broken Eddie Lee's Tech record. Eddie Lee was actually there on the sideline as Tech's assistant strength coach. After two more carries in the fourth quarter and another

Shades of Eddie Lee: In the snow, and in just over three quarters, P.J. Daniels ran for an NCAA bowl-record 307 yards against Tulsa in the Humanitarian Bowl.

touchdown, Chan Gailey sat P.J. down with about 11 minutes left.

There was no need to play him any more; Tech won 52-10. It was an incredible experience. All of which came crashing down when I walked out of the press box, slipped on the ice in the aisle, hit three steps and BAM! I landed right on my back; knocked the wind out of me. I thought, "Oh, no, I've broken my back again."

Up in the Air

At least the flight home from Boise was much better than that trip home from the Air Force game. It had been snowing during that game. The wind was blowing 20 miles an hour. It was just miserable. Afterward, we got to the airport in Colorado Springs; we had a charter flight on an old DC-8.

I was sitting next to Jesse Outlar, the sports editor of the *Atlanta Constitution*. Jesse was a little nervous. It was snowing; the pilots were thinking they could get us out, but they had to de-ice the plane. We were out on the runway, and I looked over at Jesse. He had these little miniature bottles of vodka. He was popping them open. Not being much of a drinker myself, under the circumstances I thought I might have one. I said, "Hey, Jesse, you got one for me?"

I could hear people praying, "Oh heavenly Father...." Others were saying, "Oh, we're never going to take off." I'd never thought of Jesse as a strong man, but as the

Pepper Rodgers, on a calmer flight home, brought the 1953 Sugar Bowl trophy back to Atlanta.

plane started to move, he grabbed my hand and almost crushed my wrist.

We started down the runway but then... Rummmmmppp! We stopped. The pilot said, "Ladies and gentlemen, we couldn't get up to the speed we need. But we're going to try again." People were shouting, "No, no, no!" So we went back into the terminal.

PARTYING WITH PEPPER

Pepper Rodgers was the Tech coach, and he came up to me and said, "Kim, how much money have you got on you?" Growing up, I never had that much money. One of the things, even to this day, that is consistent with me is that I keep a good bit of money on me. I pulled out my money clip and Pepper grabbed it from me.

I said, "What are you doing?" He said, "What am I gonna do with all these kids? I'm gonna find all the beer I can find and we're gonna have a helluva beer party." Pepper found a guy who got us four kegs and set it up in a bar, and we had a beer party.

You could never do that now, of course. Nobody got out of hand. Nobody got rowdy. It was just Pepper's way of rewarding the kids while we were waiting to get out of Colorado Springs.

KID STUFF

As a young boy growing up in Atlanta in the '50s, there were no professional sports, at least not major-league sports. We had the Atlanta Crackers, a minor-league baseball team that played in old Ponce de Leon Park. They were somewhat of an institution in Atlanta.

Sometimes I'd get to go to games with my dad and grandfather; we'd sit out in the bleachers. Every once in a while, they'd have races, too. Footraces.

That was the first time I ever noticed Georgia Tech.

At that time in Atlanta, you had no choice but to be a Tech fan. At Thanksgiving, Dad and Granddad would take me and my brother, Buddy, to the Scottish Rite game. It was a Tech-Georgia freshman football game that was always played on Thanksgiving morning. The game was a benefit for the Scottish Rite Children's Hospital. It was always cold on that morning, but they had the Shriners Band, and hot chocolate and cookies. We'd sit in the south end zone at Grant Field, in the old horseshoe. It was always a highlight of my year.

A BIG LITTLE FAN

I kept scrapbooks while I was growing up. In them were these wonderful pictures from the Atlanta papers, sequential photos of plays from the games: a kick return for a touchdown, or a long pass, with a drawn dotted line to help you follow the ball.

At age 12, my heroes were Wade Mitchell, the Tech quarterback, number 11, and George Volkert, number 24, the right halfback. In grade school, I wore Wade Mitchell's number and pretended I was him. I was Wade Mitchell, number 11.

One Christmas, I wanted to get a complete Georgia Tech uniform: a helmet, jersey, pants and a football. I was so disappointed when I got a note from Santa Claus: "They don't make uniforms that small."

Back then, Tech was the biggest thing in town, and going to a Georgia Tech game was a social event. People came to Grant Field all dressed up, women in dresses and hats, men in suits, ties and fedoras. They came in fancy cars. It was easy to be a fan then. Georgia Tech, and Bobby Dodd, were at their peak.

THE OLD NEIGHBORHOOD

We lived in the West End, out by John A. White Golf Course: 1694 Westhaven Drive. Our backyard ran right into the third hole. I still remember our phone number: PLAZA 5-3853. Those were some of the best days.

Here's how safe Atlanta was: A friend and I would get 50 cents each from our parents and take the trolley from the top of the street. We'd get off downtown at the Paramount Theater and Loews Grand. The Georgia-Pacific Building is now where the theaters were, on Peachtree Street.

After meeting with a worried Bear Bryant that morning, I saw Tech upset defending national champ Alabama 7-6 and celebrate what Bobby Dodd called his "greatest victory ever."

It cost a dime to get into the movie. Coca-Colas were a nickel and candy was a nickel. When we'd spent our 50 cents, we'd go home.

We never had a problem, and our parents never worried. That's how small-town Atlanta seemed to be. At the movies, during the newsreels, they had AP clips. I'd see things from different states. In the football highlights, invariably I'd see Georgia Tech.

AN EXTENDED HIGH SCHOOL RECRUITMENT

I was in the 10th grade at Brown High when Tech started to recruit me. Back then, schools could recruit anybody, at any time. There were no restrictions.

Spec Landrum was the recruiting coordinator at Georgia Tech at that time. My coach at Brown was Jack Peek. Spec wanted me to sit on the sidelines at all Tech home games.

That was huge! It was like going to Yankee Stadium, watching Mickey Mantle.

There was a restaurant, Aunt Fanny's Cabin, that was up in Smyrna. One summer, I got to go up there with some Tech players to have lunch. By the time I was a senior, I was being recruited full-time by a lot of big-time schools: Alabama, Tennessee, Florida, Georgia, Auburn, Tech, Washington, Southern Cal, Notre Dame.

BEAR TRACKS

In November of 1962, Alabama, the defending national champion, came to town with a 26-game unbeaten streak. The morning of the game, my parents, my girlfriend and I were invited to the Georgian Terrace Hotel, to Bear Bryant's suite. Alabama was ranked number one again, but Bear was worried.

He was sitting by the window. You could see Grant Field from there. He was sitting with a pack of Chesterfields and with a pack of Benson & Hedges.

He was chain-smoking, smoking one from one pack, then one from the other. He kept looking out the window at the rain, and saying, "This is Dodd's weather, this is Dodd's kind of weather."

He said, "Mrs. King, excuse my language, ma'am. But that damn Dodd's gonna beat my butt today." He said it about 10 times. My father said, "Coach Bryant, you've got a national championship team. You've got all these players back."

Bryant said, "It's raining. It's a sloppy field. This is Dodd's weather. This is Dodd's weather. He'll figure out how to play in this weather. He knows how to win in this kind of weather."

Bear was visibly worried.

He was right, too. Tech scored first after intercepting Joe Namath. When Alabama finally scored, Tech stopped them on a two-point conversion. They stopped them twice more, the last time in the last minute. Tech won 7-6. Coach Dodd always said that was his greatest victory.

IN DODD WE TRUSTED

As I weighed my college options, I considered that my brother, Buddy, was at Florida. My high school receiver, Charlie Casey, was there, too. He was Steve Spurrier's number-one receiver and made All-America. I was almost ready to commit to Florida when "Dynamite" Goodloe called.

Billy "Dynamite" Goodloe was Tech's recruiting coordinator then; he used to call me "Leh-hander." Not left-hander. "Leh-hander." Dynamite said, "Leh-hander, Coach Dodd wants to come out and see you, your mom and your dad. He wants to come out *now*." Coach Dodd came out with Jack Griffin, Tech's offensive coordinator. The entire neighborhood was watching intensely; my mother had told everyone that Bobby Dodd was coming out to our house.

Coach Dodd spent most of the time guaranteeing my parents that I might not become a great player, but I'd get a degree. I would be set, and he would take care of me. When he left, my mother said, "I told you I wasn't going to tell you where to go to school. But you'd make me very happy if you went to Georgia Tech."

Georgia recruited me heavily, too. But Coach Dodd was just too strong a man. I signed with Tech in early December, an early commitment, so I could get it over with. The chemistry between Coach Dodd and me was just too great, too strong.

WELCOME TO THE FLATS, FRESHMAN

When I got to Tech that fall, I had all these images of Coach Dodd as a compassionate and caring coach. On our first day as freshmen in pads, a manager came down and told our freshman coach, "Send Kim King, Tommy Carlisle, Scotty Austin and Haven Kicklighter up to see Coach Carlin on the defensive field." I had no idea what was going on.

Jim Carlin was the varsity secondary coach. All of a sudden, they're breaking us up into a head-on tackling drill. I looked around for Coach Dodd. I was thinking, "This is Georgia Tech. This isn't supposed to be."

Four of the guys on the defense were Bill Curry, who played for the Packers and Colts, Billy Martin, who was an All-America end, Ted Davis, who later played pro football, and Dave Simmons, who later played for the New Orleans Saints. They had us five yards off the tackling dummies, and the defense five yards off the dummies. They'd toss us the ball, we'd go and they'd tackle us.

I took as modest an angle as I could and got hit. Tommy Carlisle wasn't so modest. He was from Avondale, and my roommate. He was a fullback, and he bowed up and ran right over some guys. One of the senior players reached out and grabbed Tommy after he ran over those players and said, "You and I are going one on one."

They did, and Tommy ran right over him! The other varsity players roared. Ted Davis told Tommy, "See me in Grant Field later on, in the north end zone."

I went there, too. I sat up in the East Stands while everybody was waiting to see what was going to happen. Davis said, "Freshman, you're pretty tough. You've got what it takes." And he shook his hand. After that, nobody messed with Tommy. He was a hero. And he was *my* roommate!

TOMMY, CAN YOU HEAR ME?

Tommy became a great player, a fullback and line-backer. He played at Cleveland for a year, but was later killed in a car accident. He was on his way home from Mississippi to Cairo when a truck carrying dynamite was hit by a car. An explosion occurred. A piece of shrapnel hit Tommy in the stomach and he died several days later in a hospital in Carrollton. It was a great loss for football, and for me personally.

At Tech, Tommy always got in some kind of trouble. He'd drink a beer when he wasn't supposed to. He had a roulette wheel, and would have dice games in our dorm room. He'd buy a huge $12 bottle of scotch and sell shots for a dollar.

At certain times it was expected for me to get in my bunk bed and let my desk be the poker table. I wasn't going to tell him no.

A guy nicknamed "Possum" would stop by sometimes. One night, he didn't have a dollar for a shot, so Tommy had him drink a bottle of tequila, chug it.

About 10 minutes later, Possum started to get sick and quiver. He passed out in a resident advisor's room. While Possum was out, Tommy completely shaved him.

When he woke up, Possum was wild again. Tommy took him to Grant Field in the middle of the night. There was a crowd of students, with car lights turned on, now watching Possum running around in his underwear and an alpine hat. A bit later, he was just wearing the alpine hat. Everybody left but Possum. The campus police came and arrested him.

THE WRATH OF DODD

The next day, I got a message: "Coach Dodd wants you in his office at 11 o'clock." My heart dropped down to my toes. I knew what it was about. Tommy went in first; he said, "Don't tell him we did any gambling." I went in, and Coach Dodd had a riding crop in his hand. He never yelled at anyone.

He said, "Kim King, I've been getting bad reports about you and Tommy Carlisle. You've had gambling in your room." This was true, to a point, although I never actually participated in it. I just let Tommy do what he wanted to do. I said, "Yes, Coach, we did." He replied, "You made Dean's List. I'm gonna keep you, but kick Tommy Carlisle out this quarter. Any more trouble with you, I'm gonna tell your mother."

I'll never forget the fear that put in me, and I never did give him any more trouble.

Two

In Dodd We Trusted

My freshman year, we were undefeated, 3-0. We beat Tennessee, Vanderbilt and Georgia. I was redshirted my sophomore year. I had a bad habit of getting the ball down low, side-armed, and getting too many balls batted down. I was sent to work with Johnny Griffith.

After Georgia fired him as head coach, Coach Dodd hired him. Johnny worked with me as a special project. He did drills with me so I'd get the ball up higher. That whole year, I worked with Johnny. I got to know him very well.

Johnny was real big on the passing game. He talked a lot about reads, reading defenses, and his philosophy of throwing the ball. I did many drills with him that made me look awkward. Other players came over on the field and gave me grief. He also worked with me on raising my release point and getting it higher. He worked on my arm strength and accuracy. Evidently, it all worked.

At that time, we had really good football teams and great players. Still, one of my scariest experiences was my first start, in September 1965.

MR. SATURDAY NIGHT

The opener was at Vanderbilt on a Saturday night. As we were warming up before the game, Coach Dodd came up to me; as always, he was wearing a suit, tie, and a hat. He said, "Kimmy, you won the job, but this is your first game, we're on the road. You're probably going to be a little tight, so I'm not going to start you. I'm going to put you in, but I'm not going to start you. That OK? You sit up by me." Jerry Priestley, a senior, started at quarterback.

Tech was a very organized team. The offense always sat on one side, the defense on the other side. Coach Dodd sat in the middle, on a folding chair, with his coaches and a phone. He had his defensive and offensive captains next to him, next to his defensive and offensive coordinators.

In his autobiography, Bear Bryant said, "If I could work a football team Monday through Friday and turn it over to Bobby Dodd on game day, we'd never lose a game." He thought Dodd was a brilliant strategist. Many coaches did.

There was an aura to Coach Dodd that is hard to explain. He commanded respect; he was, in many ways, a demigod. I thought he was the smartest man I'd ever met. So, without any argument from me, Jerry Priestly started at quarterback.

Tech football was once the biggest game in town in Atlanta, and Coach Dodd was always considered one of the most brilliant sideline strategists.

BLOCK THAT KICK

Early in the Vandy game, we were going to quick-kick. Coach Dodd was a master at the quick-kick. We were in I-formation. Priestley was under center, Tommy Carlisle was the fullback and Giles Smith was at tailback. The fullback was supposed to go to the left and, with the quarterback's legs spread wide, the center was supposed to snap the ball through his legs to the tailback, who would then quick-kick.

Carlisle went the wrong way, to his right. Giles almost kicked him in the butt. I was a bit nervous. I was sitting next to Coach Dodd and I was only 18 years old.

Coach Dodd was sitting there calmly, and saw what happened. He said to Jack Griffin, "Jack, I want you to get Tommy Carlisle out of the football game. He almost got in the way. I want you to put Fred Barber in at fullback."

Coach Griffith said, "We don't have a Fred Barber." Coach Dodd said, "I want Fred Barber at fullback!" Jack turned to Lewis Woodruff and asked, "Do we have a Fred Barber?" Lewis said, "Hell, no. He's playing for Georgia. He means Ed Varner. They played together in high school."

I sat there thinking, "Good God, this man I've idolized doesn't even know his players!" Jack Griffin said, "Coach, do you mean Ed Varner?" Coach Dodd said, "Jack, that's what I said." I was totally deflated.

Put *Me* in, Coach?

A little later, after Vandy got the ball, they punted down to the one-foot line. I was thinking how glad I was that he put Priestley in when Coach Dodd said, "Kim King, get out there." I thought, "My career could be over if I fumble the snap." I ran two quarterback sneaks, and made about six inches rushing; still I didn't fumble that football! We punted on third down. I played the rest of the game and the rest of my career.

We tied Vandy 10-10, then lost our home opener to Texas A&M. After we beat Clemson and Tulane, Auburn came to Grant Field.

THE GENIUS OF BOBBY DODD

I thought Auburn was a really good team. They were fast and tough, as Auburn usually was. It was always a close game between Tech and Auburn. This was my first big game. It was a sellout, about 60,000 people. All the Auburn fans were in the south end zone. Auburn was a seven-point favorite.

I thought, "This is what makes Bobby Dodd a great coach: his ability to make his team win." I was looking to his genius to see how he would do it.

He wasn't a fiery guy, like Knute Rockne. He didn't fire you up. Yet I knew he'd have some words for us.

In the locker room, we were on pins and needles. Everyone was nervous. An official looked in and said, "You've got two minutes." We still hadn't heard anything yet. Finally, Coach Dodd spoke: "Men, Auburn's got a good football team. The oddsmakers think they're a seven-point pick. I think they're right. Playing here at home, we give 'em seven points. That's a 14-point game."

He paused. "But we're gonna beat that team today, men. We're gonna keep it close 'til the fourth quarter, and I'll figure out a way to win. We're gonna play smart. We're not gonna fumble, or throw interceptions, or make mistakes. Now, go out and beat 'em."

We did just that, 23-14.

⌘ ⌘ ⌘

Coach Dodd didn't use emotional cheerleading to appeal to us. He told us the truth and emphasized the importance of our ability to focus and concentrate, think and not make mistakes. He felt if we did, if we could get him to the fourth quarter, then he, Bobby Dodd, would find some way to make us win.

He was a master. Yes, indeed, he was a master. He'd seen how a quick-kick could work. He would notice things others didn't. He was uncanny in his ability. He could strategize better than anybody.

In my sophomore year, we played Georgia when they were blitzing all the time. We didn't have a tight end crossing pattern. Coach Dodd called our tight end over, Corky Rogers, and said, "When you see that linebacker line up here [to blitz], Corky, Kim, you have a little check-off [for a crossing pattern]."

Coach Dodd was always wearing sunglasses. Sometimes, he'd take that jacket off, but he never took off his tie. He was always calm, always thinking. He was composed and so gracious.

He always complimented the opposing team and coach. If we got beat, he never complained about officiating; he just paid his compliments to the opposing team.

A Neyland Devotee

Coach Dodd was a huge believer in the kicking game. He got that from playing for General Neyland at

Let it Snow! Lenny Snow was the 1965 Gator Bowl MVP after rushing for 136 yards and a touchdown in our 31-21 win over Texas Tech.

Tennessee. He knew the kicking game, the quick kick, won games in those days. He didn't have a very prolific offensive system by today's standards. We would usually throw 15 times a game. It was the kicking game that kept us alive.

If Coach Dodd could keep the opponents on their side of the field, the more chance they'd make a mistake—an interception, or a fumble. Or our punt returner might make a big return.

TECH VS. TECH

At the end of my sophomore year, we played Texas Tech in the Gator Bowl. They had a great back in Donnie Anderson but had just lost to Arkansas. Arkansas won the Southwest Conference championship and went to the Cotton Bowl. Texas Tech went to Jacksonville, to play us in the Gator Bowl.

During practice all week, nobody thought that we'd be able to run against Texas Tech, that we would have to throw every down. When we got to the game, Coach Dodd called us up and said, "Men"—it always sounded like "min" to me—"this is a good football team. They've got a great player in Donnie Anderson. Men, if we win the coin toss, we'll kick." All of the players said, "What?"

He said, "I watched them in warmups. They're tight." On the second or third play of the game, Donnie Anderson fumbled. We scored, and they never recovered from that. We rushed for 364 yards and beat them, 31-21.

Right after the game, Donnie Anderson signed the biggest contract ever at the time with the Green Bay Packers. He had a cigar, and he signed the contract standing right under the goalpost.

"The Gray Fox." That's what people called Coach Dodd.

DODD THE DISCIPLINARIAN

Earlier that year, when Navy came to Atlanta, it was the first time an African-American would play at Grant Field. We had a kick returner named Jimmy Brown. He was from Chattanooga and little, just 165 pounds. He was fast, though, like the "Pony Backs" Tech used to have.

The entire time leading up to the game, Coach Dodd was preoccupied with good sportsmanship. He didn't want anything to happen that would reflect badly on Georgia Tech. The summer before was the time of the Selma riots, Montgomery, Bull Conner in Birmingham. Desegregation had just hit the South. It was a very tense and uncertain atmosphere.

Early in the game, Navy punted the ball. Jimmy Brown caught it, and it was like Moses parting the sea. A Navy player tried to catch Jimmy, and it was like a thoroughbred and a mule. We had a player from Alabama, who was all excited and agitated. There was no way this African-American was going to catch Jimmy Brown, but our guy made a legal block, peeled back and just really hit him. It was legal; no flag.

It's the only time I ever heard Coach Dodd curse a player. He came out on the field and got on him and really chewed him out. It said a lot to me about Coach Dodd's care, compassion and dignity. He wouldn't allow his teams to run up the score, or embarrass or cheap-shot an opponent.

⌘　⌘　⌘

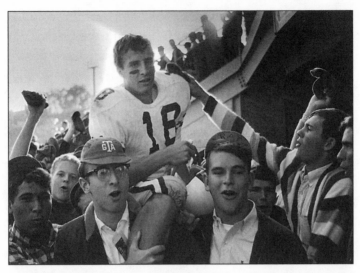

I got a free ride off Grant Field after we beat No. 8 Tennessee 6-3 in '66. Somehow, **Sports Illustrated** *even named me its national player of the week.*

We played Duke that year for homecoming. We had a pick play that was barely legal, that we might use down on the goal line on fourth down. That day, we had two wide receivers in the slot, Mike Fortier and Craig Baynham, our flanker. At the goal line, Baynham ran off Fortier's pick.

I think I threw three touchdown passes in the game. We were running out the clock with Lenny Snow carrying the ball. We were down inside the 10, and I couldn't resist running that pick play. Bill Murray, the Duke coach, was absolutely livid.

In the locker room, Coach Dodd called me into his office. He said, "You played well today, but don't do that again. You should never make your opponent look bad when you're up comfortably. If I was the quarter-back, I'd have taken a knee and run out the clock."

I took that to heart. He did not want his teams to humiliate an opponent in any way. He wasn't mad, though. There is a trite, old expression that "football tests character." He felt that you could learn many lessons from football that were about more than just winning and losing.

Coach Dodd was a brilliant strategist. He had street smarts. He knew how to win. But he also had a great deal of compassion and character. He didn't want us to lie or be disrespectful to people. He was a good man. They called him "The Gray Fox."

AN EXCEPTION

The only time Coach Dodd deviated from the dictum to not run up the score was in the opening game in 1966 against Texas A&M. Gene Stallings was A&M's head coach. It all went back to the Darwin Holt-Chick Graning incident in the '61 Tech-Alabama game— Holt's vicious hit on Graning that Coach Dodd insisted was intentional.

Stallings had been the defensive coordinator for Alabama in that game. Coach Dodd said in a *Sports Illustrated* article that before the Tech-Texas A&M game, Stallings was "disrespectful" for calling Coach Dodd's offense "simple", but mainly for saying Tech's players were soft, not hard enough. That really upset Coach Dodd. He told the team that there are many big games, but this one meant a lot to him.

He said, "I've never asked a team to win for me personally, but I'd really like to win this game." We didn't play well in the first half, and we were losing 6-3 at the half. We made some adjustments at halftime, a staple of Dodd teams. We won 38-6. Late in the game, I was thinking Coach Dodd would call it off. But his admonition was, "Run it up." Those weren't his words; he didn't tell us that, and maybe it's my imagination. But after never running it up, never embarrassing your opponents, I think that was a bit of revenge for him.

Near-Perfection in '66

We were undefeated, 9-0, after we beat Joe Paterno and Penn State 21-0 at Grant Field. I had broken my right hand that year in the Tulane game. I basically broke it in two and had to have a bumblebee cast on it. However, I made it back for the Georgia game.

Georgia had one loss, 7-6, to Miami with Ted Hendricks. They had Bill Stanfill, George Patton, Edgar Chandler, and Billy Payne. Back in those days, on the day of the game we used to take the train to Athens.

We'd get dressed at Georgia Tech, then take buses to Emory, where there was a train station right on campus. We'd have our cleats on, our game pants on, our game jerseys. We'd carry our shoulder pads and helmets, and wear warmup jackets.

The train took us right behind Sanford Stadium. We'd get off at the station, walk down the steps, go into the locker room and put on our shoulder pads and jerseys, then go play. We did that my redshirt season, but my junior year was the first time Tech didn't take the train to Athens.

We rode buses.

By 10:30, we hadn't left Atlanta. There were no interstates at that time. It was an hour and 20 to 30 minutes to Athens. Everybody was very nervous, asking, "How are we going to get there in time?" Hugh Hardison [once Tech's longtime security chief] was with the state patrol then. Coach Dodd finally came down and said, "Okay, men. Hugh? Get 'em on the bus."

We went out 78, Memorial Highway, by Stone Mountain. The state patrol had every intersection blocked off. We were on three buses, going 70 miles an hour. We never stopped. The state patrol escorted us and we got there in an hour. We immediately got dressed, but I noticed Coach Dodd got in Hugh Hardison's car and drove off.

I thought, "What's that? That's not like Coach Dodd before a game. Maybe TV has him on." Years later, I was having dinner at his house after a Tech game, and I asked him, "Do you remember that game at Georgia? We took buses, and you took off with Hugh Hardison. Where did you go?"

He said, "Let me tell you, Kimmy. There's the best little hot dog stand by the airport in Athens. Better than the Varsity. I said, 'Hugh, take me over there and let me get two toasted hot dogs!'" That's the kind of man, and coach, he was.

Coach Bryant used to throw up before games. Not Coach Dodd. Hugh said, "I had to walk in with him. It was this little ol' shack, and I was afraid somebody might have a knife or pull a gun on him."

The trip back was very long; Georgia beat us, 23-14.

I was stunned when Coach Dodd retired shortly after our 1966 season and the Orange Bowl loss to Florida.

LIFE WITH DODD

Coach Dodd hated long practice sessions. Also he didn't want his players to kill each other and cause unnecessary injuries in practice.

On Saturday, we played the game. On Sunday, we'd take a steam, get a massage, but no practice. We'd watch the game film from the day before. On Monday, we'd go out in sweat bottoms, jersey, shoulder pads and helmet, but we didn't hit. He didn't believe in *any* contact in practice once the season started.

The coaches would run through plays our next opponent would run, maybe for 30 to 45 minutes. We'd do some light jogging to loosen up. On Tuesday it was full pads, an hour and 45-minute practice but still no hitting. On Wednesday we did the same thing.

Quarterbacks *never* got hit. We wore a purple jersey that meant "Don't hit."

On Thursday, we were dressed like on Monday: no hitting, an hour practice. We'd polish up the kicking game. On Fridays, we were out in the stadium in sweats for maybe 30 minutes, polish up. The players played touch football. On the road, we'd go out and take in the stadium, get a look at it. On Saturday we played.

OUT OF SEASON

In the off season, Coach Dodd would go to Bitsy Grant Tennis Center every day and play tennis. He couldn't stand the cold, though. He'd play checkers every day, too, with Bitsy Grant and the other guys. One spring day, he invited me and Jimmy Brown out to play tennis. We were thrilled he asked us to play.

When we got there, he told us to sit down and watch while he played checkers. He waited 'til he saw the sun at a certain angle, then said, "Okay, let's go."

I figured we were going to kill these old guys; Coach Dodd was always playing doubles with some doctor. I said to Jimmy Brown, "Take it easy on them." Coach Dodd said we'd play for a dollar a game, "With one condition: We get to pick the side of the court." That was just fine with us.

He had us play on the side looking directly into the sun. Coach Dodd had this scoop shot, a squat move where he'd bend his knees and hit this two-hand dinky shot about 30 feet into the air. We couldn't see the ball with the sun in our eyes and couldn't return anything. They destroyed us. It was humbling—but that was Bobby Dodd. He figured out a way to win before he ever started playing.

A Lemon of an Orange Bowl

We scored the first touchdown in the Orange Bowl. We flanked Craig Baynham wide left, hooked him inside, and I hit him. I wasn't sharp that night, but Florida wasn't really good, either. I don't think anybody on either side of the ball played that well.

The game went back and forth. In the third quarter, we had Florida backed up on their six-yard line.

Steve Spurrier ran a draw play to Larry Smith. We had a safety blitz. However, our safety, Bill Eastman, ran to the wrong side. When Smith broke through the line, he outran the secondary.

But his belt broke! He ran down field, holding the ball in his right hand and holding up his pants with the other! He went 94 yards to score.

Larry Good came in for me, and we ended up losing 27–12.

The next night, January 2, we had a banquet at a country club in Miami. I had a date with the Orange Bowl queen. What I remember, though, is dancing with Mrs. Dodd. We always had a good time together.

True to Georgia Tech form, we flew back to Atlanta that night, and had to be registered for classes the next morning. They cut us no slack; we went from the Orange Bowl to academics the next morning. That was the Georgia Tech way.

A SHOCKING RETIREMENT

I always assumed Coach Dodd would be at Tech at least through my career there. But a few weeks after the Orange Bowl, I picked up the paper and read that he was retiring.

I was crushed. He was the major reason I went to Georgia Tech. I think after losing the game he felt he wasn't on top of his game anymore and needed to retire.

I went to his office where his longtime secretary, Margie Bennett, let me see him. I said, "Coach, you didn't tell us. We didn't know anything." He said, "When you're not as strong, when you're not as energetic and focused as the guys around you—your opponents—you're not as good."

He was 63 when he retired. He'd won 165 games [165-64-8]. I think he had at least five good years left in him. He could've easily won another 35 or 40 games to break 200. I admired him for that.

I hated it, too, of course. He stayed on as the athletic director, but I wanted to go out with him as coach. Again, he was the reason I went to Tech. He had a system of not working yourself to death. He had the support of the city. He had a recruiting network, had great players and talent. He was happy at Tech. He wanted to keep getting results.

But as is typical of Coach Dodd, he used his retirement as an example: "Most people, they hang around too long, in a job, a profession. You need to know when to quit. It's time for me to quit. I've had a great run. It's time to step aside and let a younger guy take over."

He didn't ever want anyone telling him when it was time to quit.

JIMMY, BOBBY AND BEAR

Years later, Coach Dodd was talking to an alumni group. Jimmy Carter was there. Coach Dodd said, "Mr. President, we're so proud of you. I know you're having a tough time with those Russians in the Cold War. But if you send me over to Russia, with my old friend Bear

Bryant, I'll come back with all their missiles, and Bear will come back with all their vodka."

It was pretty well known that Bear liked his vodka. The president got a big kick out of that.

OFF-THE-FIELD FOLLIES

During my freshman year, there was a guy named Jimmy Stringer who had a place called "The Piedmont Drive-In Club." Not the Piedmont Driving Club. It was on Piedmont Road, where the Squire Inn is today.

Jimmy had told the freshmen, "If you beat Georgia, I'll close down the Piedmont Drive-In Club for you." We beat Georgia and he closed his club. On a rainy Monday, we had a beer party there. Joe Auer was a senior. Billy Paschal, who went to Sylvan High School near me when I was at Brown, was there, too. After a few beers, Joe decided to take a trip.

He had an uncle, a veterinarian in Decatur. He had alligators and a pet tiger. Joe came up with the saying, "Put a tiger in your tank." Esso bought that from him. Joe kept an alligator under his bed in the dorm. It was about three feet long; he kept a collar on it. That gator could snap your finger off. One time, a maid almost had a heart attack when she found it. She turned Joe in.

That Monday, we went to the vet in Decatur. He had a young tiger that was about three feet high and four feet long, and 80 pounds or so. He had enormous feet and paws. They threw him in the back seat of the car, with me, and he had *not* been de-clawed.

The tiger started ripping the back seat. I said, "Joe, your tiger back here is ripping up your car." The only thing I hoped was that he stayed occupied with ripping up the seat and didn't rip me up. Fortunately, he didn't. We drove over to the Piedmont Drive-In Club to show off the tiger.

Back at the School...

Later, we drove back to Tech for dinner at the dining hall. Freshmen ate at 5 p.m. Everybody brought back beer. Helen Twiggs was the dietician; she always said she took care of "Her boys." That night, though, she got upset over something and called Coach Dodd.

Coach Dodd was a great guy, but he didn't get close to many of his players. He was very fair, but very firm. He'd say, "I'm gonna *far* 'em." Not "fire," but "far." That was his favorite saying: "Kim King, if you don't stop doing that, I'm gonna *far* you."

He came right over to the dining hall, but the players had been told he was on the way, so we high-tailed it to the Varsity for dinner.

The next day, he called a team meeting. He had that riding crop in his left hand; he kept hitting it in his right palm. He gave us a tongue-lashing, said, "I'll far all y'all." Fortunately, nobody got "farred."

AN UNCOMMON JOE

Joe Auer later played with Buffalo, then the Miami Dolphins. However, when I was a freshman, Tech played LSU at Grant Field. Jerry Stovall ran back a kick return for a touchdown, and LSU won 10-7. Late in the game, Billy Lothridge threw a long pass to Joe, who dropped it. On TV afterwards, they asked him, "What did you say when you dropped the pass?"

"Whoops!" Without blinking an eye, Joe said, "Whoops!" A lot of players were mad, but those who didn't play thought that was funny. That was Joe: funny guy, didn't take things seriously.

Three

A Sad End and Happy Return

Who to Hire?

Up until 1966, Georgia Tech had effectively had only three coaches: John Heisman, Bill Alexander and Bobby Dodd. It is hard to believe, three coaches in 63 years. There was a great deal of speculation and many rumors at the time. The players were on pins and needles. We couldn't find out any information.

Frank Broyles, who'd coached under Coach Dodd, was asked if he'd be interested. He declined in order to stay at Arkansas. I found out later that a decision had been made on Bud Carson.

The president of Georgia Tech, Ed Harrison, and Bob Tharpe, a former letterman and All–SEC tackle on the athletic board, had met. Alexander and Dodd had both come up from the staff when their predecessors

Coach Alex: Tech's 63-year coaching trinity of Heisman, Alexander and Dodd included William Alexander, who won 134 games and the 1928 national title. As Tech's head coach from 1920-44, his 25-year tenure was the longest in school history.

had retired. Bud had one year as defensive coordinator at Tech. Bob Tharpe recommended that they hire from within the staff.

Differences in Style

With Bud, it was a different style. Coach Dodd tried not to over coach, not to be too technical. He preferred a player use his natural instincts in playing. Fundamentals were important, but were not to override your instincts. Bud's approach was more fundamental, a technique approach.

Coach Dodd was supportive; he rarely fussed, hollered, or got on players. Bud was more a Marine drill sergeant; he'd get on guys, rarely being supportive.

There was a tremendous contrast between the guys who were recruited by, and fit into the style of Coach Dodd, and those of Bud.

All of a sudden, overnight, we were cast into this boot camp mentality where players were fussed at more and made to practice more. The practices were more physical. Very candidly, not many players adapted very well, especially the seniors.

A Long, Losing Season

We won our first three games but lost six, ending up 4-6. Tech hadn't gone 4-6 since 1946, Coach Dodd's first season as head coach. A bad year for Dodd would be 6-4.

I tore my ankle up in the Clemson game and missed four whole games. The next week in Knoxville, I wasn't planning to play against Tennessee, but they needed me.

I couldn't push off on my ankle after taking a snap or when I was going to plant and throw, so they put me in

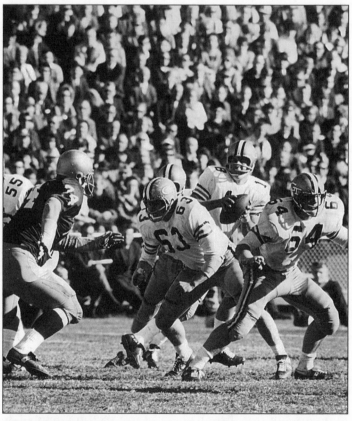

After Coach Dodd's retirement, I struggled under Bud Carson my senior year.

a shotgun formation. I got hit from the blind side, and my ankle was really bad. I missed three more games.

All in all, it was a very bad season. Not just from a won-lost standpoint, but the atmosphere. There was an air of tension and hostility that existed between the players and the changed coaching staff.

Bad Karma

To use a phrase, it was just "bad karma." My sophomore and junior years, I called 90 percent of the plays myself. Carson wanted to call every single play from his hand signals. I not only had to learn the game plan, I also had to learn the hand signals, which changed from game to game. He changed them because he was afraid people would pick them up.

I remember thinking, "Golly, dog." I had this tough academic schedule, had to study intensely, and at the same time, learn these hand signals and the game plan. We still had plenty of good players: Lenny Snow, Randall Edmunds, David Barber, Eric Wilcox, John Lagana, Tommy Carlisle and others. It was just a bad season. The whole thing left me in a less than enthusiastic mood about playing pro football.

NO TO THE PROS

I was drafted in the ninth round by the Pittsburgh Steelers, and I played in the East-West Coaches All-America Game in Atlanta that summer in Atlanta-Fulton County Stadium. However, my senior year had soured me on playing pro ball.

I regretted that decision not to play pro ball for five years, maybe 10 years. Looking back, I'm glad I didn't do it. It enabled me to get involved in a career—real

Bill Fulcher (right) coached just two seasons, won the 1972 Liberty Bowl behind backup quarterback Jim Stevens (left), but then quit.

estate—and to establish my own company in 1972, Kim King Associates, Inc. Had I gone into pro football, I would've started my business career much later. I think it's worked out very well this way.

My senior year seemed to be a bit traumatic. Here was a group of seniors, who'd gone to the Gator Bowl and Orange Bowl, won our first nine games as juniors and went 9-2; then we lost six games my senior year. To this day, it still bothers me.

A FOOTBALL SEPARATION

I did distance myself from Tech for a few years. I felt like there was some tension. I graduated in March, and I didn't leave with a good feeling for Tech.

Carson had one winning season in five years and then got fired. When Bill Fulcher came in, I got involved again a little bit. I eventually re-engaged with Tech.

A CHANGE OF COMMAND

Fulcher had played for Coach Dodd in the mid-'50s, and he was hired as head coach in 1972. That was the start of the Eddie McAshan years, the first black quarterback to play at Tech.

In his first year, Fulcher took Tech to the Liberty Bowl. This was when Jim Stevens started at quarterback, after McAshan was suspended. He threw three touchdown passes, and Tech beat Iowa State 31-30. He was the MVP. Stevens became Tech's director of academic services.

After spring practice the next year, Fulcher went to Coach Dodd and said, "I think I want to step down." Coach Dodd replied, "You don't do that now. You don't step down in the spring, or just before the season starts." Coach Dodd told Fulcher he had to coach another year.

After that season, Coach Dodd, George Mathews, George Morris and Larry Morris approached Frank Broyles about coming back to Tech. They couldn't get him to do it. In the process of talking to Broyles, he told the group, "You guys don't have the right administration in place to give a coach a chance to win. Only one coach in the nation can overcome that and win: Pepper Rodgers at UCLA."

They went to talk to Pepper at the coaches convention in Houston, and he took the job.

PEPPER

Pepper came back and was an immediate lightning rod for positive change. He came in with a permanent in his hair and no socks. He rode a motorcycle to work, and he brought the wishbone to Tech.

His '74 team went 6-5. He had some good players: Jimmy Robinson. Danny Myers, David Sims, and later Eddie Lee Ivery. Pepper's offenses were great, but his defenses couldn't stop people.

Love that perm: The flamboyant Pepper Rodgers returned to his alma mater as head coach in 1974.

For three or four years, Pepper had the support of a lot of people. There were many others who didn't support him. Most people who weren't Pepper supporters felt that off the field, he wasn't what Georgia Tech football should be.

For several years, there was tremendous pressure, and rumors and innuendo floating around. People were trying to get him to resign or get fired. Eventually, the athletic board made the decision to terminate him.

KIM KING, BACK ON BOARD

By then, I'd been on the Tech athletic board for several years. Back in 1974, Taz Anderson, Joe Delany and I had helped form an "ad-hoc" Yellow Jacket Club. We were very unhappy with the direction the Tech administration seemed to be taking the football program. There seemed to be no direction, no leadership for the program.

Coach Dodd was still the athletic director, but Joe Pettit was the Tech president. Dr. Pettit wasn't a big football supporter at all. This was after Tech had left the Southeastern Conference and before they had joined the ACC. There was talk about Tech football being de-emphasized, and even some talk about Tech becoming like Princeton and joining the Ivy League.

Our ad-hoc Yellow Jacket Club had no standing, no official status. But about 300 people showed up, just by word of mouth, at the old Royal Coach Hotel at Howell Mill Road and I-75.

They were not very happy people. Some of them even said, "Let's go fire the president!" All of them were good, solid Tech guys, or at least 90 percent were. They just wanted to get Tech back on track.

Dr. Pettit took that as a real threat. He heard about it, and called me and asked, "What's all this about this group?" I said, "This group doesn't feel like there's much administrative support for football." To subvert that threat, he asked me, "Well, why don't you come on the athletic board?" He might have thought that was a way to control me. I replied, "That would be fine."

We, the football supporters, wanted a voice.

If You Build It...

After being on the athletic board for several years, I always closed the meetings by asking Dr. Pettit when Tech was going to modernize its athletic facilities.

He refused to address my concerns until one day, in a pique, he said, "I'll make you chairman of a committee to investigate the feasibility of building this new athletic complex. But you have to remember, we have to raise the money ourselves; we get no state help."

I said, "Definitely, that's fine." I went home that evening and called Coach Dodd to say, "Coach, we've done it. We've got a feasibility study group put together. I'm chairman, and I want you to be our honorary chairman."

He said, "I want to think about it. The economy's bad. The administration really doesn't want this project to succeed. And I'm not sure it'll work. I'll call you in the morning."

The next morning, he said that not only would he not do it, but he didn't want me to do it. He thought we'd fail.

In frustration, I called Dr. Pettit and said, "Dr. Pettit, I'd like your permission to step down as chairman to vice-chair and let me bring in Ewell Pope, one of Coach Dodd's former players, to be chairman. Dr. Pettit said, "Fine," and I called Ewell. He said, "I'm traveling to China on business and really don't have time." I said, "Ewell, you really only have one job, and that's to get Coach Dodd to be the honorary chair."

He replied, "No problem." Two weeks later, he called me and said Coach Dodd wouldn't do it.

THANK YOU, MR. PRESIDENT

Hugh Carter, a Tech graduate and good friend, was at that time a special assistant for administration under President Jimmy Carter, his cousin. From time to time, Hugh and I would chat about Georgia Tech and how things were going. It was during one of those calls that I told him of the predicament I was in, and that Coach Dodd would not agree to be our honorary chairman.

Hugh said, "I just got an idea about how to help you on that. I'll be getting back in touch a little later with my plan."

Two to three weeks later, I got a gold, engraved invitation from President Carter to be his guest at the

Coach Dodd (with All-American Larry Morris and the 1955 Sugar Bowl trophy) used his charm to raise money for Tech's Edge Athletic Center.

White House. I wanted to go with Coach Dodd and George Mathews. We flew up in George's private jet from Peachtree-DeKalb Airport.

There was bad weather that morning; I drank two or three cups of coffee. Coach Dodd turned to me and said, "Kimmy, I want you to go to the bathroom."

I said, "Sir?"

"Yes, I want you to go to the bathroom," Coach Dodd said. "You've been drinking a lot of coffee. It's going to be a bumpy flight, and you need to go to the bathroom now, on the ground, rather than up there during the flight." I did what he said and it was a good thing. The flight was very bumpy. He was right. That was the kind of man Coach Dodd was: very observant. He could see things other people could not.

A meeting in May of 1979 at the White House included (L to R), me, Hugh Carter, George Mathews, Bobby Dodd and President Jimmy Carter. (Official White House photo)

The West Wing

We landed at National Airport and the Secret Service came out to meet us with a limousine. They took us to the White House, to the West Wing. There was a Marine security guard, and Hugh Carter gave us a tour. We met vice president Walter Mondale, who was ecstatic to see Coach Dodd. He went to the University of Minnesota and knew of Coach Dodd. He acted like a child at Christmas.

We saw Rosalyn Carter, and finally got to see President Carter. We walked into the Oval Office, and the president jumped up, ran across the room and bear-hugged Coach Dodd. He said, "Bobby Dodd, one of my great heroes, someone I've always admired. So glad to have you here."

We talked, and then the president said, "By the way, Coach, we need a new athletic complex down at Georgia Tech. If they ask you to get involved, would you do it for me?" Coach Dodd said, "Yes, Mister President, I will."

Hugh Carter was standing behind Coach Dodd. When Coach Dodd said yes, Hugh was winking at me as the plan he'd conceived worked. I've often thought of the many people who were key in getting that athletic complex built. But I feel Hugh Carter was very responsible, because he delivered Coach Dodd's commitment.

On the plane home, Coach Dodd told me, "Damn you, Kim King, you and that Ewell Pope. You weren't men enough to get me to say yes. But I couldn't say no to the president of the United States."

LET THE FUNDRAISING BEGIN

Our first solicitation was in Houston, to get some big money to start the campaign. Keep in mind, this was in the mid-'70s and we had to raise the funds for the athletic complex externally. There were two big oil money guys, and one big international construction guy. These were three of Coach Dodd's old friends.

One of them met us at the airport. He was wearing this inexpensive, old white shirt, with a string tie that was stained. I thought, "Who is this gardener they sent to pick us up?" His car was about 15 years old, a real clunker. He drove us to the Houston Oaks Country Club.

I had the plans for the athletic complex. Doug Weaver, Tech's athletic director, was there, too. The entire lunch meeting revolved around Coach Dodd and his friends reminiscing about old times, old games. Finally, Coach Dodd made his pitch to the three of them. One said, "Bobby, I'll give you five hundred."

Another man said, "I'll give five hundred, too." The third said, "Two-fifty." I'm adding this up. I'm thinking, "That's $1,250." I was ready to unload on Coach Dodd. It's the only time I ever got mad at him. He said, "What?"

I said, "Coach, the damn plane tickets alone cost us $1,600." He put his hand on me and said, "Oh no-no-no-no-no, Kimmy. I think they're talking about a million and two hundred and fifty thousand dollars." I was floored, so embarrassed.

Sure enough, a little old check came in from one, then the other, then the third. That's the kind of magic, and appeal, Coach Dodd had for Tech people. They'd do anything for him.

A FULLER APPRECIATION

Later on, as we drew near the end of the fundraising, we only needed one or two million dollars more. We approached Fuller Callaway. He went to Tech, and was a great Tech fan. He'd come to Atlanta on the train from LaGrange to go to Tech football games.

He said, "I'll close out the campaign on one condition: I want the building named for my long-time personal assistant and manager, Arthur 'Skin' Edge."

That's how it came to be called the Arthur B. Edge, Jr. Athletics Center.

Four

PEPPER TO CURRY
TO ROSS

FINDING PEPPER'S SUCCESSOR

A search committee was formed to find the next coach. I was on it, along with Bill Schaffer of the school of management, Bill Sangster, the dean of the college of engineering, Doug Weaver, the athletic director, and Tom Daniel, a football player. We were the search committee.

We were in New Orleans, at the national coaches convention, and we held the interviews in my room. We interviewed Bill Curry, Larry Travis, Jerry Glanville and the coach at Southern Miss who later went to SMU and got them on probation, Bobby Collins.

Afterward, we went to dinner at Antoine's. I'll never forget Dr. Pettit ordering a gin gimlet with onions. I'd never seen anyone order a gin gimlet with onions.

Over the course of dinner, he polled the people on the committee. It was obvious we were going to hire Bill Curry.

Bill Curry came home to Georgia Tech in 1980 and turned the program around—only to leave for Alabama after the '86 season.

FAVORING CURRY

Larry Travis was a solid candidate, coming off of Pepper's staff, and would have been ideal for keeping continuity.

Jerry Glanville was naturally very self-confident. And Bobby Collins was just coming into his own at Southern Miss before later going to SMU. SMU was placed on NCAA probation for rules violations in its football program.

The committee felt that there had been a lot of dissension building during the latter years of Pepper Rogers's regime, and thought it was important to bring in someone who could understand not only the importance of Tech's athletic tradition, but who could unite the alumni. Even though he had no previous head coaching experience, Bill Curry was the unanimous choice of the committee.

I knew, and had played with, Bill, and knew he would work hard to rebuild Tech's support. I also felt that it would be a rocky road until he got his program established.

A ROCKY START

Bill's first year, 1980, got off to a rocky start. Tech lost to Alabama at Legion Field, 26-3. Alabama was ranked No. 2 and was the two-time defending national champ.

Mike Kelley was Tech's starting quarterback for the third straight year. That team won only one game, lost nine and tied one. Tech ended up losing to Georgia, with Herschel Walker, a freshman, at tailback. The tie was with Notre Dame, who at the time was No. 1.

HEAVES AND FISHES?

There was a great exaggeration by the media that fans pelted Notre Dame's sideline. I'm sure there was a fish or two thrown, but not anything like the debacle reported by the media.

Watching Georgia Tech fight and tie Notre Dame 3-3 on a field goal late in the game was one of the most remarkable performances I've ever seen by a Tech team. Totally outmanned, with few skill players and a noticeable lack of speed, Tech played hard-nosed defense, made play after play after play when needed, and shut down the No. 1 team in the country.

With the final score 3-3, I always felt like Notre Dame tied Tech and not the other way around. That same day, Georgia beat Florida on the "Run, Lindsay, Run!" last-minute pass from Buck Belue to Lindsay Scott. So, by virtue of Tech's tie with Notre Dame, and Georgia's remarkable season that year with Herschel Walker, Georgia ended the season as national champion.

A GOOD SECOND START, BUT...

The 1981 season started out with great promise. Robert Lavette, just a freshman, started at tailback. In his first game, he had a tremendous rushing day against Alabama, including two touchdowns. One came late in the game, to give Tech a 24-21 upset of fourth-ranked Alabama at Legion Field.

Lavette's winning touchdown was set up by a 54-yard, third-down pass from Mike Kelley to Ken Whisenhunt, the tight end who is the only Tech player ever to earn six varsity letters. Alabama fought back and tried a last-play 50-yard field goal, but it fell short.

The next day, Bear Bryant said, "The only player I wanted was that little number 20." That was Lavette. "He beat us by himself."

Tech rejoiced after freshman Robert Lavette ran for two TDs to upset Alabama 24-21 in the 1981 season opener—Bill Curry's only win in his second year.

AN IMPERFECT 10

Lavette didn't beat anyone else the rest of the season, though. Tech didn't win another game, lost 10 in a row, and finished 1-10. It was Tech's worst season in modern times, since John Heisman became the coach in 1904.

That season, Notre Dame got revenge in South Bend, 35-3. It probably would've been easy for everyone to blame it all on Bill Curry, but the fact is that he had very limited talent and very poor team speed on both sides of the ball.

Every Monday, Bill would go sit down with Coach Dodd and let Coach Dodd critique him. I remember Bill on numerous occasions, and even to this day, telling me those were the toughest sessions he ever sat through. It killed him to lose, but I knew he was determined.

⌘　⌘　⌘

Taz Anderson was a good friend and great tight end who went on to become the NFL Rookie of the Year with the St. Louis Cardinals. He and I went to Bill after his second disastrous season and suggested that he go out and hire nationally outstanding offensive and defensive coordinators. Bill got a little irritated with us, but finally admitted that it was a question of money, that he didn't feel like he had it in his budget.

That's when Taz and I and 18 others raised money—$200,000—for enhanced salaries for the coordinators. Bill eventually hired Rick Lantz on defense and Dwaine Painter as the offensive coordinator.

It was tough to be a Tech fan during those days. The media piled on. There was very little support, other than from our quarters.

In 1982, Tech finally had a winning season, at 6-5. I think the reason was that Bill Curry had a chance to recruit better players. He had a little more experience as a head football coach, and certainly the two coordinators he brought in—Lantz and Painter—were able to make great contributions, offensively and defensively.

But '83 was another letdown. Tech finished just 3-8 and didn't win any games outside the Atlantic Coast Conference in its first season playing in the ACC.

WELCOME TO THE ACC

Tech's entry in the ACC was certainly an interesting story in itself. Back in the '70s, when it was obvious that Tech needed a conference affiliation, an overture was made to the Southeastern Conference about rejoining.

Bear Bryant endorsed the move and told Coach Dodd he would do everything in his power to try to pull it off. Eventually, several of the SEC schools voted it down.

Next, an inquiry was made to the ACC, but at that time it was known more as a basketball conference. A lot of Tech people were not pleased with the direction Tech took. But Doug Weaver, the athletic director, did a marvelous job of negotiating Tech's entry.

NO WOLFPACK TICKETS

Doug was holding out for the ACC to admit Tech without any payment or compensation. Willis Casey, then the athletic director at North Carolina State and the person appointed to negotiate Tech's entry, countered Doug by saying, "Doug, I'm tired of negotiating. N.C. State will give Georgia Tech the $100,000 to $150,000 to join the conference. All we ask is that Tech give its ACC basketball tournament ticket allotments to us for five years to repay us."

Doug, after further thought and research, finally went back to Willis and said Tech would be glad to pay the money, but it would keep its ticket allotment.

It's been a good affiliation for Georgia Tech. Now, with the expansion of the conference to 12 teams, including Miami, Virginia Tech and Boston College [and eventually 14, then 15 teams], it will certainly be one of the stronger football conferences in the country.

Also, the ACC affiliation gave Tech added standing for bowl appearances. Furthermore, the money contributed during the basketball tournaments have been substantial sums.

THE TURNAROUND FINALLY BEGINS

In 1984, Curry finally turned the corner. Lavette was a senior, and Tech won its first three games, including Alabama in the opener and Clemson. Tech was even ranked for awhile, and went 6-4-1. Don Lindsey, the

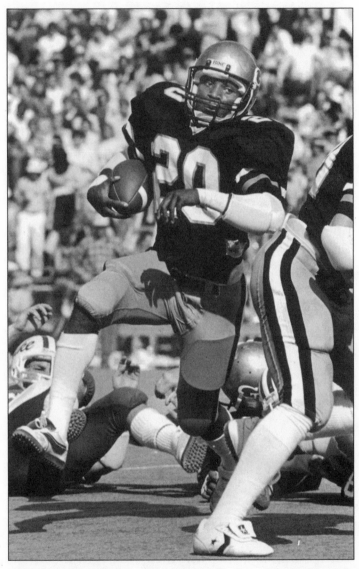

Robert Lavette, Tech's career rushing leader with 4,066 yards, helped launch Georgia Tech's turnaround in his senior season of '84.

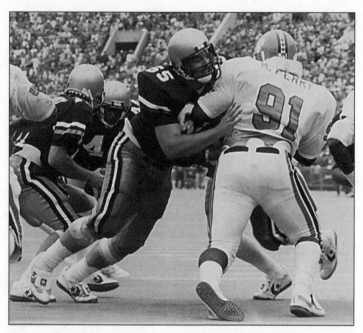

John Davis (65), "The Refrigerator Mover," was also a great Tech pocket protector.

new defensive coordinator, was a great coach and instituted "The Black Watch Defense."

The 28-21 win over Clemson ended Clemson's 20-game ACC winning streak. Tech led 21-0 but needed Chuck Easley's touchdown in the last 30 seconds to win it.

John Davis, Tech's center, was called "The Refrigerator Mover." That's when William "The Refrigerator" Perry played for Clemson. The key was whether or not Tech could block him. John Davis enjoyed a great day, and earned the sobriquet, "The Refrigerator Mover."

Tech made few mistakes, and played superb defense, particularly down near the goal line. I recall an outstanding goal-line stand. It all contributed to that big victory over Clemson.

At Blessed Last...Georgia

The final game in Athens was one of the few times that Tech beat Georgia during that period. Tech had lost six straight games to UGA. Malcolm King ran a fullback trap for one of the big plays of the game, for some 60 or so yards, and Tech went on to score and take control of that game.

Trapped! Malcolm King's (29) long burst on a fullback trap helped Tech trounce Georgia 35-18, its first win between the hedges in 10 years.

John Dewberry scored on a quarterback draw, and Tech won for the first time in Athens since 1974, 35-18. All in all, it was probably Curry's biggest victory.

Tech stopped its losing streak, and subsequently the ridicule from Georgia fans. The media started to recognize Georgia Tech and Bill Curry as having a pretty good football program.

And in '85, it was a real good team.

SAKES ALIVE, '85!

That was the year Gary Lee ran the kickoff return through the fog that night against Georgia. Gary Lee, the "Galloping Ghost from Dougherty County," ran it 95 yards back through the fog for a touchdown to beat the Dogs 20-16.

That was the night where he scored going all the way from the South to the North end zone. I remember that game well.

Afterward, they tore down the old wooden bleachers in the South end zone. I thought several times during the game of having sat in the South end zone as a kid with my father, grandfather and brothers, watching the Scottish Rite games. I've still got a piece of the bleachers as a souvenir that I keep in my den.

That victory wasn't sealed until late in the game, though. When Georgia was driving, their quarterback, James Jackson, was hit and fumbled the ball. Tech recovered to clinch the win.

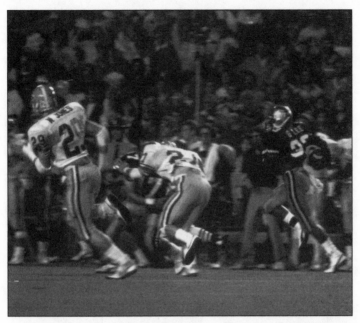

Onward through the fog: Gary Lee's 95-yard kickoff return through the fog beat Georgia 20-16.

In addition to Gary Lee and a stunning performance by John Dewberry, the guy who contributed most, I thought, to that win was Ted Roof. He was a linebacker and one of the captains of that team. Roof wasn't expected to play, having severely sprained his ankle. He couldn't push off on it. After Georgia continued to run inside with their big back, Lars Tate, who later played pro football, Ted begged to play later in the game.

He finally got in. With great guts and courage, and with total disregard for his own body, he shut down Georgia's inside running game.

To me, that was the difference in Tech's win, controlling the inside running game.

Later Duke's head coach, linebacker Ted Roof keyed Tech's great "Black Watch" defense in 1985.

THE INTRIGUING MR. DEWBERRY

John Dewberry was an interesting story. Heavily recruited by Tech, he chose Georgia. After a year or two, he decided to transfer to Tech because he didn't feel like he'd be given an opportunity to play quarterback at Georgia.

Watching him early in his transfer year, I was not impressed with his arm strength or throwing ability. But there was something about John that made him a winner. He knew he could get it done, and he could get others around him to get it done, too.

After he began playing and starting, he became an outstanding quarterback. John had street smarts and could talk anybody into almost anything—including talking me into hiring him when he graduated, even though I'd told him several times that I didn't have a spot for him in my company. He's now a very successful real estate developer in Atlanta.

GOIN' BOWLIN'

I was at my farm in Coweta County when I heard that Curry had disciplined John Dewberry, sent him back home and wasn't going to play him against Michigan State in the All-American Bowl in Birmingham. Curry picked Todd Rampley, a sophomore who hadn't played much all year, to play quarterback.

I drove over to Birmingham on New Year's Eve with Beau, my son, and did the game with Al Ciraldo. I recall that Curry told me that George Perles, the Michigan

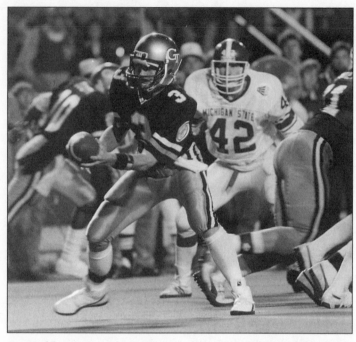

In Todd we trusted: Replacing the suspended John Dewberry, quarterback Todd Rampley helped beat Michigan State in the All-American Bowl.

State coach, had asked him, "Why would you send your best player back home and diminish the game and play your second-team quarterback who hasn't played much all year?"

But Todd Rampley did a great job. It was his first career start. He didn't make any big plays, but he didn't make any mistakes, either. He scored Tech's first touchdown and Malcolm King scored the last. Tech beat Lorenzo White and Michigan State 17-14.

BIG CHANGES

In '86, Tech went 5-5-1. But several weeks later, I got a call at my office from Bill Curry. He said, "Kim, I want you to know before you read it in the *Journal-Constitution*. The University of Alabama wants to talk to me about the head coaching job. I'm going to talk to them."

Ray Perkins had left Alabama to go to the Tampa Bay Buccaneers. My response was, "Bill, why would you talk to them?" He said, "Well, I guess I'm flattered; it's Alabama, Coach Bryant."

Later, Coach Dodd told Bill, "You can stay at Tech as long as you have competitive teams. You don't have to go undefeated or win the ACC. You can stay as long as you want. But you can't win a national championship. If you want to compete for a national championship, Alabama's the best place to go. They can compete for it every year."

Their president, Joab Thomas, had a mission of changing the image of Alabama from a football school to an academic school. He'd hired Steve Sloan from Duke as his athletic director. This was a big cultural change for Alabama. Thomas felt Curry fit his image of what he wanted at Alabama.

MEMORIES OF CURRY

I'd known Bill Curry since before I was a freshman at Tech. He'd played at College Park High, and I had great admiration for him—for his toughness and competitiveness. He was an overachiever on the field, and seemed to always rise to any level of competition.

I remember the first spring practice I went through. I ran a sweep against the defense. Bill really hit me hard from his linebacker position, so hard that I had a hip pointer and was pretty well knocked out of spring. I'll never forget peering up at him from the ground and seeing him gritting his teeth down at me, although to this day he denies he did it.

That was Bill, though: a great guy off the field, but a fierce competitor on it. He's now one of the outstanding television commentators, and still one of my good friends. He's meant a lot to me, as a mentor and a great example of what a leader's all about.

RE-STARTING OVER

Bill took the Alabama job, and the process started over. This time, Homer Rice was on board as the athletic director. Homer always had a backup plan for a backup plan. The coach he wanted was Bobby Ross.

Ross had left Maryland after the Len Bias brouhaha. Bobby left and went to Buffalo to coach the offense and Jim Kelly at quarterback. At Maryland, I think Bobby felt he got a black eye from the basketball program, with Lefty Driesell and Bias's death. They [Maryland's administration] left Bobby dangling, and he left. Bobby's a very principled man.

George O'Leary came from Syracuse to coach the defense. Ralph Friedgen came from Maryland, where he

Bobby Ross, in a rare pose during his first two seasons—smiling.

was on Bobby's offensive staff. The first year they won only two games, the second year three. Tech didn't win an ACC game those first two seasons.

There was a lot of grumbling by Tech alumni. Bobby Ross is a tremendous coach and wonderful person. However, he is not a warm person in the sense that he has a lot of friends and opens himself up to fans and supporters.

As a result, many questioned whether or not Tech would be able to win with Bobby and George O'Leary and Ralph Friedgen. How wrong they were.

A SPURRIERITY COMPLEX

In Bobby's first year, Duke destroyed Tech in Durham. Steve Spurrier was coaching Duke and was up big late in the game. It looked they were going to empty the bench. Not Steve. He was throwing the ball. He hit a couple of bombs, and they scored again to make it 48-14.

That's when the scoreboard flashed, "Welcome to the Basement Tekkies!" I felt anger and resentment. I will always remember Coach Dodd saying: "You don't need to pour it on."

To me, it was a real rub in the face. Some people say it was because Spurrier was passed over to replace Pepper. I don't know. Steve never said.

A WAKE FOR THE EATING

Two games later, Tech lost 33-6 to Wake Forest. That was the night Ross came home, got in his car and drove around and around I-285, listening to Christmas carols and thinking, stopping only to get ice cream.

He felt he couldn't coach, couldn't get it done. He was all doom and gloom. He almost quit. But to his credit, he didn't, and he *did* get it done.

After the season, I went to see Bobby because I was concerned about his emotional and physical well-being. I knew he had poured his heart and soul into the job, and also knew that he had great questions about whether or not he could get the job done at Tech.

I suggested to Bobby that he and Alice, his wife, make a trip anywhere in the world, and several of his friends would pay for that trip. Bobby's response was that he didn't like to travel, period.

Next, I said, "Well, take a golf trip with a bunch of your buddies and, likewise, we'll send you wherever you'd like to go." Bobby's response was, "Well, I don't play golf." Tennis? "Nope. Don't like tennis."

Totally frustrated and exasperated, I said to Bobby, "Well, what do you really like to do?" His answer was this: "I like it when school is out in June [Tech was on the quarter system then] and I can then come into the office, bring a sack lunch of two peanut butter and jelly sandwiches and a Budweiser, and come in early in the morning around seven o'clock and watch film all day, enjoy my lunch, not be disturbed by anybody and go home at 6:00 p.m."

Having heard that, and realizing how focused Bobby was and how much of a workaholic he truly was, I stood up, simply shook his hand and said, "God bless you, Bobby," and left his office.

TURNAROUND II

It took another whole year, of course, to get back on the winning side. But in 1989, the little running back, Jerry Mays, who'd torn up his knee and missed the 1987 season, rehabbed and became, I think, one of the best runners Georgia Tech ever had.

When Jerry injured his knee, he was told by the coaches that he was too little to play running back because he wouldn't be able to block.

Jerry was the most determined player I think I've ever seen at Tech and was key in the turnaround for Bobby Ross and his football team.

Being short, he ran close to the ground. Jerry had tremendous quickness and speed, but not great break-away speed, as some thought. He'd hit a hole as quick as anyone and was absolutely fearless.

After losing the first three games, Tech won seven games. Yet Tech's failure to get a bowl bid really frustrated and angered many people. They closed out the season with a really good win over Georgia at Grant Field, and I know the players and coaches were angry. It gave them a great incentive for that off-season, that spring and the next year—their national championship year.

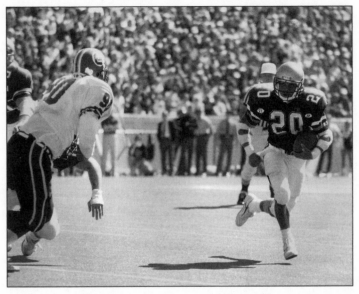

Little Jerry Mays (20) overcame a knee injury to become one of Tech's greatest backs and helped Bobby Ross's program turn the corner.

Bobby Ross had turned the corner. And his teams were not only good, but they knew they were good. They played with a swagger, something that all good teams have to have.

Five

THAT
CHAMPIONSHIP
SEASON

O ne of the keys that typified the 1990 team that became the co-national champion was the way they closed the previous season. They played with a great swagger and self-confidence. They were very physical and were confident they were going to win. As the season went on, you could see that confidence grow.

What really spurred that team on—the nucleus of that team—was the fact that they didn't get a bowl bid after finishing 7-4. They were a very good football team. That was really the launch-pin, so to speak, of the next season. There was an attitude of, "We're gonna show people that we're a worthy team."

THE FIRST TEST: NO CONTEST

I guess the first big game they had that year that really challenged them was Maryland. They were undefeated and Tech was an underdog. It was a night game, and Mark Duffner was Maryland's coach. Tech just took them apart, 31-3.

Then Tech beat Clemson, 21-19. At that time, Clemson was beating Georgia Tech pretty regularly. It was a very physical, tough football game that, I think, gave great confidence to that Tech team.

THE ONLY BLIP

Then came the frustration of going on the road to Chapel Hill, where Tech hadn't won since 1945—the year I was born and when Frank Broyles was the quarterback at Georgia Tech.

The frustration that day: Tech got down to the goal line, took four shots, tried to get it into the end zone, but couldn't punch it in from a couple of yards out. North Carolina put up a heck of a stand. That 13-13 tie was really deflating.

But they hadn't lost. By the time Tech got to the Virginia game, I knew this was a special team. Number one, you had a great quarterback in Shawn Jones.

SHAWN JONES

If there's one word to describe Shawn Jones, it's "escapability." He had the ability to go back in the pocket and, if the pressure caused the pocket to break down, he had not only quickness and the smarts to know when to pull the ball down, but he was strong physically. He could push off of people.

He'd get caught up by people, and he could stiff-arm or push people off. He had enough strength to do that. He would take a busted play and turn it into a sizable

A four-year starter, Shawn Jones showed the ability and "escapability" to become one of Tech's greatest quarterbacks.

gain—or at least positive yardage, just about every time. Very rarely did he get sacked. He was a very confident and poised quarterback.

Ralph Friedgen helped him tremendously. Shawn had started as a redshirt freshman. He was very athletic, but he didn't have that good arm early. I think through Ralph's coaching, he was able to improve his reads mentally. That gave him a chance to know where to go with the ball early in a play, and helped him become a great quarterback. And he was a great one.

THE TOP TECH QBS

I would say Shawn Jones is easily among the top five quarterbacks of all time at Georgia Tech.

I'd also add Billy Lothridge, who could do everything—pass, run, punt, place-kick. He finished second in the 1963 Heisman Trophy voting to Navy's Roger Staubach.

Another great one is Joe Hamilton, who started for four years, holds nearly every Tech passing and total offense record, and who was second in the Heisman his senior year.

I'd put George Godsey in there, too, because of production. There was a kid who wound up when he threw the ball. He was not a smooth, natural athlete-type of performer. George was so smart on a football field, and so quick with his reads and getting the ball to the right place. It was almost like he willed himself to be a great quarterback.

A quadruple threat, Billy Lothridge was second in the 1963 Heisman Trophy voting behind another quarterback—Navy's Roger Staubach.

I think he eventually ended up being one—really with only two years of eligibility left. He sat on the bench all that time when Joe Hamilton was starting, and played very rarely.

Back in Coach Dodd's era, there was Wade Mitchell. Wade was a very mechanical quarterback. Tech didn't throw the ball more than eight or nine times a game back then; they had so many great running backs and great offensive lines. Coach Dodd didn't believe in throwing the ball unless he needed to.

Wade was a 4.0 student, very smart, very tough, very savvy on the football field. Not a great passer in the throwing sense; but then again, there weren't a lot of great throwing quarterbacks at Tech in the '50s. Coach Dodd's teams didn't throw the ball that much.

When I played, we didn't throw the ball more than 15, 16, or 17 times. That was a big game, to throw 17 passes in a game. Now, these guys throw 35, 40, 45 times a game.

Those would probably be the top five quarterbacks whom I've seen play. There have been a lot of good ones who didn't make the top five, but those would be my five best.

The Virginia Game

So, here's Virginia, undefeated and number one in the country. They've got Shawn Moore, a great quarterback, and Herman Moore, the great wideout. They had the big running back, Terry Kirby. It was a typical George Welsh well-coached football team.

His offensive coordinator was Tom O'Brien, who's now the head coach at Boston College [and later N.C. State]. George had a great staff and a very powerful football team.

They were not only good at the skill positions, they were very physical, very big.

Tech has always struggled in Charlottesville. I don't know why. It's a strange phenomenon. You can look at every team, and there's one opponent they struggle against on the road.

We used to go down to New Orleans when I played, and we'd play Tulane every year. Not to disrespect Tulane in any way, but we were always much better than they were. But we had some of our closest, most difficult games with them. It just seems that certain teams rise to the occasion, and certain teams play an opponent and sort of go off the charts.

It's the same thing with Virginia. They don't play well down here in Atlanta. So you wouldn't think the home field would continue to be that much of an advantage. But it's turned out to be that way.

THE SETTING

It was such an exciting environment in Charlottesville. There was national television, all this media. They had a blimp, the Sea World blimp, painted like Shamu the Whale, circling over Thomas Jefferson's university. I wonder what Jefferson thought of that?

The night before, some students had a bonfire out on the field and burned part of the Virginia logo off the artificial turf. I don't know if it was Tech students, as some people said, or if it was just a bunch of partying Virginia students who got carried away.

Nevertheless, it was funny to see the field. You had this big patch out there; they got it from the leftover turf from Virginia's baseball field, and sewed it in. The grass and the fibers and the color didn't match up. Maybe on the field it wasn't that noticeable, but up where we were, it really looked out of place.

Early that morning, they even wondered if they'd be able to play the game. They were worried about those seams, ankles getting turned, knees torn. But they were able to play.

I remember the crowd was one of the most festive crowds I'd ever seen. They always are at Virginia. At that time, they had the bowl end, with the bank of grass. They had all those students in there, and they were jammed in the stadium. They had not done the expansion yet. But it was a really good crowd by Virginia standards—probably 50,000 and maybe 1,000 Tech fans.

THE BEGINNING

Virginia was a heavy favorite, and the game started out exactly that way. Virginia just really pummeled Tech in the first half. It was 28-14 at halftime. Al Ciraldo asked me at halftime, "What about the second half?" I said,

"Al, Tech has to make a big play early in this quarter and has to get some points and get back on the board, or Virginia's going to run away with this game."

Lo and behold, on the first play of the second half, Shawn Moore was trying to run an option and got hit and fumbled around his 20. A play or two later, Shawn Jones hit Jerry Gilchrist, the track star, on a pass behind the corner and that made it 28-21. Then Tech tied it up.

Virginia won the first half, and Tech won the second half. Tech finally took the lead midway through the fourth quarter, but eventually Virginia tied it up at 38-all. With a little over two minutes left, Tech started the drive that led to Scott Sisson's field goal.

THE DRIVE, THE KICK

People have asked me, ever since, was Sisson's kick the biggest play? Was Shawn Jones's run, on a scramble for a touchdown, the biggest? To me, the key play in the game was a third-down call on that last drive. Virginia was in a two-deep, and Shawn Jones hit William Bell coming out of the backfield on a circle route. He ran a circle over the middle just trying to get behind the linebackers, who were dropping in coverage.

The linebackers were in really good position. But Shawn threw the ball high, which was the only way he could throw it. Bell went up and made a great one-handed catch. As soon as he caught it, he was hit. But it was enough for a first down and kept the drive alive.

Scott Sisson (9) and the Jackets rejoice over his game-winning field goal.

Several plays later, with seven seconds left, Sisson kicked a 37-yard field goal. And Tech had won, 41-38.

THE EXULTATION

How did I feel? Giddy. It took me back to my child-hood. I was almost like a kid again. I was thrilled.

I had taken a private plane up with some of my friends and former Tech players who played with me. We were like kids. It was just one of those glorious days when Tech had come in and beaten the number-one team in the country, a darned good team, and had done it under tremendous pressure. For Scott Sisson to hit that field goal, to me that was one of the great games I've been fortunate enough to see Georgia Tech play. It was just totally exhilarating.

WELCOME HOME, JACKETS

When the Tech team came back to campus, it was late at night—11, 12 o'clock. When the buses came down Techwood Drive by the east stands to let the players off, they couldn't get in because the students were out in the street. They'd torn the goal posts down on Grant Field and were parading them around campus.

They had a huge student outpouring, and everything coalesced around that game. The Tech community, all the people who were the fence-sitters, the people who would go either with Georgia or Tech—whoever was winning—the subway alumni, if you will, it seemed everybody was on board. And everybody was talking about Georgia Tech football.

Everybody knew this was a special team. I remember thinking how proud I was of Bobby Ross, and George O'Leary, and Ralph Friedgen. The first couple of years, those guys took severe criticism from Tech fans. To turn that program around—and not only turn it around, but win a national championship in four years—was remarkable.

ISN'T IT IRONIC?

The irony of all this goes back to what Coach Dodd told Bill Curry. That is, "Bill, you can stay at Georgia Tech as long as you want. You don't have to win 11 games a year, or beat Georgia every year. Tech folks will love you, and you can stay here. But if you want to compete for a national championship, you can't do it at Tech. You have to go to Alabama."

That was irony. That was four and a half years after Coach Dodd told Bill that.

STILL, A SHOCKER

Truthfully, I'd had my doubts that Tech could ever contend for another national championship—only because I knew the academic stress Georgia Tech places on students. There are certain players, like defensive linemen, in most cases where the great ones are semi-animals. School isn't that important to them.

Don't ask me why, and I'm not trying to pick on defensive linemen. There have been some smart ones and some good ones. But by and large, the "War Daddies," as I call them—the guys down in the trenches, the guys you go to war with—are not Phi Beta Kappas. And they don't want to be Phi Beta Kappas.

With that limitation, knowing that those guys would not only have difficulty getting into Tech but staying in Tech, I just didn't think Tech would be able to recruit the defensive talent to be able to dominate games like a lot of the guys who'd played at the interior defensive line positions for other teams.

No, I didn't think Tech would compete for a national championship, under the current setup. So I was as shocked as anybody. Did I think Tech could be really good, and be a Top Ten team? Yes. I thought Tech had a chance to do that. Not year in and year out. But I did think they could be a Top-25 team and program. And I still think that's the case at Tech.

WHAT A DEFENSE

On that defense, Coleman Rudolph, Marco Coleman, Jerrelle Williams, Calvin Tiggle, those players were fantastic. Then you had the big nose guard, Kevin Battle, "The Battleship," who kept things clogged up in the middle. He was one of Tech's first 300-pounders.

They had good cornerbacks. They had "Big Play" Willie Clay. I thought those guys, particularly Coleman Rudolph and Marco Coleman, were as good at their positions as anybody else who'd ever played there at Tech.

Coleman Rudolph was a skinny outside linebacker when he came to Tech from Valdosta High. He could run. They knew they had to play Coleman, and they felt like he could do better at the down position, defensive tackle. So they bulked him up and got him up to about 260, 265, and with his moves, he was hard to block.

Then he developed some strength; not only did he have the moves and speed, he had some strength to go with it, so that he could really be a great player. He was All-America, and a well-deserved All-American.

Marco Coleman came from an eight-man football team program in Ohio. He was not heavily recruited, yet he was one of the toughest, smartest defensive ends that Tech's ever had. You very rarely saw him getting out of

Marco Coleman broke the Georgia Tech sack record and went on to play in the NFL.

position. His technique and his play were the kind that led to big plays and solid play at his position.

He wasn't a guy running crazy and getting caught upfield on a pass-blocking scheme, with somebody running inside of him. You never saw Marco make those kinds of mistakes. He had a lot of sacks. In fact, he broke the Tech sack record, and then Coleman tied his record later.

AND ON OFFENSE...

The key to that offense was not the great Shawn Jones, or the great William Bell, or those great receivers. It was that offensive line—Mike Mooney, Darryl Jenkins, Joe Siffri, Jim Lavin, Billy Chubbs. I thought that was one of the better offensive lines in the last 20, 25 years. They were big and very physical.

That was about the time when the rules of pass-blocking changed. Players could now use their hands inside. That changed the dynamic of offensive line play. Before you needed slim-hipped, quick-feet, very agile, mobile linemen who could pull and get angle blocks and so forth. And who were also very athletic.

Now, all you needed was big bulky guys who, to be very candid, were fat. But they were very powerfully fat. They'd get their hands on you and control you because they could hold inside. Nobody called anything. As long as you kept your hands inside your shoulder pads, guys would reach out and hold and put their hands on you. When I played, that would've been holding. Our linemen were taught to hold your jersey, and don't let your hands get out any further than your jersey.

I thought that was the key to the offensive side of the ball on that team, a dominating offensive line that opened up the running game against just about everybody.

AND YET...VIRGINIA TECH

Frank Beamer brought his Virginia Tech team down to Atlanta the next week, and Sisson had to kick two fourth-quarter field goals. Tech won 6-3 in what was a terribly boring football game. Neither team played well. Yet Tech did what they had to do to get by.

Normally, if you look at a big game where a team plays great, it's sort of natural to have a little letdown the next week unless your opponent is another nationally ranked team. Virginia Tech, while they were good that year, wasn't ranked. So it was very disappointing, but it was a win. And I think it displayed the character of that team. They did what they had to do in the fourth quarter of a terrible performance and beat them with those two field goals. When Bobby Ross and the Jackets won 42-7 at Wake Forest the next week, Tech had its first ACC Championship.

TO ATHENS, AND BEYOND

The finale was Georgia, in Athens. The game began

It was pure joy when Tech trounced Wake Forest 42-7 and brought home its first ACC championship.

with Georgia taking control. They were really fired up and led 9-0, but Tech came back. Bobby Rodriguez, the receiver, made some big plays. Shawn Jones hit him with some passes. William Bell played well. Defensively, Tech came up with some big plays and ended up dominating the game in the second half and won going away, 40-23.

At that point, everything that had to work for Tech to move up in the polls worked. Notre Dame had moved up to No. 1 in late November, but lost to Penn State. That knocked them out.

Then came the bowl pairings. Tech drew a very average Nebraska team—good, but not a great Nebraska team—in the Florida Citrus Bowl. By their standards, it was a very average team. A Top-25 team, but not a dominant, Tom Osborne-coached team that won national championships.

A ROSY CITRUS BOWL

Tech just dominated in that game. Offensively, defensively, in the kicking game, they dominated Nebraska. I'll never forget the last touchdown Tech scored. Al Ciraldo described the play this way: "And Jones hands to William Bell off tackle, and he's STACKED up and he's hit and he's churnin' and he's not goin' anywhere." By this time, Bell had broken out of the pack, hit the sideline and Al was going from mundane—"And he's STACKED up inside"—to, "...And there goes William Bell!!!" He's turning it up about five decibels: "He's running down the sideline! William Bell is gonna go all the way!!! Kim King, hey, Kim King, this William Bell, a great run!"

I said, "Right, Al, you called it all the way."

AN ORANGE BOWL HEARTBREAK

At the end of the game, all of a sudden we're looking at Colorado and Notre Dame playing in the Orange Bowl. We were staying at the Peabody Hotel, and had a whole ballroom reserved for Georgia Tech—the team, the official party. We were down there watching the game on a giant-screen TV, rooting for Notre Dame.

If Notre Dame beat Colorado, then Tech was the logical choice to move up to number one. The play I remember most was the punt return by Rocket Ismail, for a touchdown late in the game. It got called back because of a clip. Everybody went from a high to a low.

Colorado won, and I thought, "Uh-oh. The chances for being number one are going to be tough to over-come."

NUMBER ONE

But the next day, the AP and UPI polls came out. There was Tech first in the UPI and Colorado, with one loss, first in the AP. It was a co-national championship, and it was incredible. It was one of those times when it seemed like a fantasy, that it wasn't happening. It was just hard to believe that it was really happening.

Everyone was totally thrilled. I remember there was a parade back in Atlanta for the team. I rode with Al Ciraldo. It was a big thrill to me—not so much the fact that I was in that parade. The thrill for me was to see so many people lining the way who were excited about Georgia Tech. It really was an affirmation that there were so many Tech supporters who, I guess, came out of the woodwork at the last minute and showed their affection for the co-national champion.

I was driving down to Georgia Tech when I heard that Tech had won the UPI national championship. I was going to the Athletic Association, because I'd talked

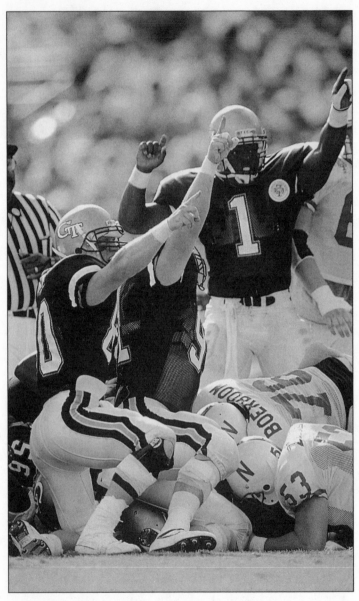

Defensively dominant and offensively explosive, Tech ran away from Nebraska 40-23 in the Florida Citrus Bowl.

to George and Ralph earlier in the day. They were really adamant that it would be an injustice if Tech didn't win that co-national championship.

I think it was George who said, "Come on down, we're gonna be down here all night." I was driving on the Downtown Connector, getting off at the North Avenue exit, when I heard it on the radio.

It was a great, great thrill, and a remarkable coaching job and performance by that team.

As a result of that co-national championship, Frank Roper, the registrar at Tech, told me that Georgia Tech broke its record for the number of student applications for admission.

I thought back to the day of Joe Pettit, and reflected: This IS important to Georgia Tech. The culture and tradition of football and athletics has always been important to Tech people. This was an affirmation of that, and it was a good feeling.

It made all those years of struggle, of getting beat by a lot of not-really-good teams and being harassed by Georgia fans and the media, worth it.

To the point where, you know? This thing worked. It had a great result, because of the hard work and commitment by a lot of good Tech folks.

Bobby Ross poses with the 1990 national championship Trophy UPI Coaches.

Six

GOODBYE BOBBY, HELLO BILL

The next year was sort of a disappointing one. Tech went 7-5, then beat Stanford in Hawaii in the Aloha Bowl to finish 8-5. It was the only Tech game I'd missed since 1974. Tech was going to cut back on its travel, and neither Al nor I went.

We did it by TV at home, with a telephone hook-up—including the postgame interviews. I did it in Gail's office outside our den. At that time, we had a wide-screen TV. I think Al was at his house, so we had to be careful not to talk over each other. We had only one line, one feed. We both sounded like we were in a can. But that's what we were asked to do, and that's what we did.

THE PIZZA BRAWL FALLOUT

That incident in the off season following the national championship, when some Tech players were involved in a brawl at a pizza place off campus, was a contributing factor to Bobby Ross leaving Tech.

Bobby had an attorney investigate the whole incident, including talking to some of the participants. It was his firm belief that his players' version of the story was the truth. The provocation was on the students' part who were in the pizza place, and not, as reported, the players brutalizing and beating up a young guy and his girlfriend.

As a result of that incident and the media coverage that slanted it to suggest that Tech had a bunch of animals who went out preying on people, beating people up and bullying them, some of the older Tech alums were really concerned about the image and quality of athletes. Some of them really put the pressure on athletic director Homer Rice.

Bobby perceived that whole situation as evidence that he didn't have the core support of the administration.

He was a very loyal guy. He expected loyalty, demanded it from the people around him: his players, his coaches. Likewise, he gave 100 percent of his loyalty to his boss and the administration. He felt like that trust had been broken.

BACK TO THE NFL

Bobby wanted to go back to the pros as a head coach, but he was very careful about who he wanted to coach for. He wanted to make sure he went not only to the right owner of a team, but the right general manager.

Art Modell, whose team was in Cleveland then but is now in Baltimore, made an overture and pitch to Bobby. Ernie Accorsi was the general manager, and Bobby had great respect for Ernie. But he didn't feel like the position was good in Cleveland, so he declined it.

Bobby Beathard, San Diego's general manager, made a run at Bobby. While Bobby wasn't sure about ownership —he didn't know anything about Alex Spanos—he

After great success at Tech, Bobby Ross made San Diego Super.

had great respect for Bobby Beathard. Bobby took the head coaching job with San Diego.

That was a big disappointment to the entire Tech community. To see a man who had struggled early—many questioned whether or not he'd get it done—but he'd turned the program, around won a national championship, had a pretty good year the next year, was poised to have another good year and team; and yet he left at the pinnacle of his success.

ONCE MORE, STARTING OVER

I think Tech's struggles in football after Coach Dodd were largely due to a lot of turnover in the head coaching position. Every time you change head coaches, I don't care if you're the greatest program in the country or the worst, it's almost like you give up two or three years.

There's new chemistry, a new philosophy. Coaches look more critically at the existing talent and start saying to themselves, "The heck with these guys. I'm going to bring my players in. The alumni will give me a pass if I don't win enough games this year."

We had all those coaches—Carson, Fulcher, Pepper, Curry, Ross—five coaches from 1967 to 1992. Five head coaches. If you assume that two years, on average, are pretty much "chuck it" years for each new coach, that's 10 years worth of squandered opportunity. Ten years out of 26 years. I think that is a big part of why Tech struggled during that period.

FINDING A SUCCESSOR

When Bobby Ross left, I felt very strongly that Homer Rice needed to give the job to George O'Leary. He was coming from the staff and had been in the program for several years, so it wouldn't be totally starting over.

George was a little rough around the edges. He'd never been a head coach—not at the college level—but I told Homer, "You can help him become a good head coach and help him with his PR."

George was a pretty gruff, pretty tough, not-gonna-waste-your-time, not-gonna-waste-my-time kind of guy. He could be very blunt and demanding and to the point. But I knew that one, George had greatly contributed to the national championship season, which was something to really recruit off of. Two, George was tough, and his players were tough. Three, if George got the job, Ralph Friedgen would stay. And I wanted Ralph to stay, because Ralph was out of the same coaching mold as George.

Ralph was a brilliant offensive guy, and George, I think, was a brilliant defensive guy. So it would be a continuation of the program. You wouldn't lose one or two years with a new coach.

ANOTHER BILL

When Bobby Ross left, Homer had a backup plan. He was disappointed that Bobby left, but he felt the program had reached a national stature and that he could recruit a nationally renowned coach.

Through the interview process with the athletic board, Bill Lewis—the national coach of the year that season at East Carolina—impressed everyone so much that they immediately offered him the job. Ralph Friedgen and George O'Leary had been overlooked and were offered jobs with the San Diego Chargers, which they both took.

Bill Lewis and his staff didn't have the respect of the players from the Ross program, and there was a big letdown in performance. Later on there was some strife with the quarterback situation between Tommy Luginbill, a junior-college transfer, and Donnie Davis, who was recruited by Ross. I remember Ralph telling me, "If I can work with this kid, in four years he'll be an All-American."

They really believed he had that much talent, but Davis struggled. And there was a lot of tension and a lot of dissension. The whole experience was not a good one. Also, there was never a uniting of the alumni and fan base. Things got worse, and it all went downhill.

DEFENSE-LESS

Bill had come from a defensive background under Frank Broyles at Arkansas and Vince Dooley at Georgia. It was quite surprising that Tech's defense was just getting hammered during Bill's time at Tech.

I would do a *Quarterback's Corner* radio show with Homer. We'd tape it during the week and it gave me an occasion to spend some time one on one with Homer.

Homer and I had developed a good respect and appreciation for each other. I said to him, "Look, I don't know if Bill is going to make it. What are you going to do?" He said, "I'm not ready to pull the plug on him." I said, "Well, you've got to get him some help on the defensive side of the football. You've got to get him a defensive coordinator, somebody who can come in and really get them to play defense."

COURTING GEORGE

Homer said, "Who do you think?" I replied, "Go get O'Leary." He said, "George is not going to come back. He wanted the head job." I said, "I've been talking to George off and on. I know this: George would like to come back to college. He doesn't like the pros."

George had told me when he was with San Diego, one of his defensive linemen wasn't using the right technique or rush lane during practice. George kept having to correct him. Every time, George was getting more frustrated, and his voice was rising. Finally, the lineman turned to him, used a lot of profanity and said, "I'm leaving. You can have this job. And by the way, they're gonna fire you. They're not gonna fire me 'cause they're paying me too much money." And he walked off the practice field.

George said, "I knew then I didn't want to be in this game anymore."

So I talked to George and said, "How would you feel about coming back to Tech?" He said, "As head coach?" I replied, "No. As defensive coordinator." He said, "That's ridiculous. I'd never consider that."

I said, "Well, just think about it." He said, "No. If anything happens and Bill Lewis is not there and that job opens up, I'd be very interested."

We talked over the course of several weeks. Finally, George said, "Okay, it's gonna cost a lot of money."

I asked, "Why don't you tell me what you want? All I can do is take it in and see if it will work."

We worked around some parameters. I said, "Would you sign a letter of intent if I drew it up?" He said, "You can't do it for Tech." I told him, "No, it'll be on my stationery, my company letterhead: Kim King Associates, Inc."

He said, "You're in the real estate business." I said, "There's no law, no NCAA rule that says I can't hire the best defensive coach in America for my company." George said, "Well, if you're crazy enough to do it..."

So we actually did the letter of intent, with George being the defensive coordinator at Tech and with all the perks—the car, the country club membership, radio stipend, just a list of things—on my letterhead. And he signed it.

I went to Homer and said, "Here it is. If you don't get Bill Lewis to hire him, I'm going to be laughed out of Atlanta as the only real estate guy in the city, if not the country, who's got a defensive coordinator on the payroll. Who the heck's he going to teach defense to?"

Lewis finally called George, who flew in and they hit it off. George assured Bill, "I'm not here to get you fired. I'm here to help you win. I'm not going to get involved in politics. I'm just going to coach defense, and I'm going to win for you. That's all I want to do. If you're here for the next 15, 20 years, great. If I get a head coaching opportunity, I'm going to leave. That's what I want to do."

With that understanding, thankfully, I got off the hook with the company. And Tech signed George and brought him back.

Seven

GUYS, I'VE GOT TO GO HOME

I still remember the date like it was yesterday: Friday, May 21, 1999. I was in Myrtle Beach, on a golf course. I was 53 years old and, I thought, in good shape. I was playing in a foursome with, among others, Taz Anderson. And I hurt my back.

Although I had been having more back pain than usual lately, that day when I woke up it was severe. I took three or four Advil before we teed off. I tried to play through the pain, as football players do. We had a big Calcutta going, two-man teams. I felt I had to play through for my partner, Ed Jones.

On the fifth hole, I hit a drive and dropped to my knees. I felt like something had decompressed, like my body had just caved in. I knew I'd injured my back; I didn't know I'd broken it. I said, "Guys, I've got to go home."

Carl Farris, a longtime friend from childhood, helped me get my stuff together and get on a plane back to

Atlanta. On the flight home, and for many months afterwards, I was in agony.

A BROKEN BACK

It turned out I had cancer. The tumor, called a plasma cytoma, was located on my T-10 vertebra, and it had caused the bone to weaken. The torquing of my back while swinging a golf club resulted in a compression fracture.

For a 53-year-old guy, I had always taken good care of myself, except for the Cuban cigars I enjoyed on weekends. I was jogging four, five times a week, lifting light weights and hunting a lot. Gail and I were traveling, enjoying life.

I had no warning signals. I had a physical every year and my blood work was always normal, except borderline anemia. I felt great.

The first appointment I made was with a Georgia Tech orthopedic back specialist. He took an MRI of my back and said I had bone spurs and some arthritis—fairly typical for an athlete. Unfortunately, he chose the wrong area of my back to check. A couple of weeks later, I had my yearly physical with Dr. Thorne Winter. On the chest x-ray, Thorne noticed the fracture on my spine and called me for more tests.

"Kim, this is Thorne." For 25 years, Thorne has called me at home at night with the results of my physical exams. He sounded different.

"I got your tests back, and we're going to have to do some more testing. We need to get these tests done immediately."

"Thorne, you're scaring me."

He assured me that we would discuss everything in a couple of days when we had a diagnosis. He set me up with Dr. Kenneth Braunstein, a noted hematologist-oncologist in Atlanta. On Tuesday of that week, I had my first bone marrow aspiration and biopsy.

The results would take a couple of days.

I didn't get much sleep that night. I can tell you how many molecules of paint there are on my bedroom ceiling. I stared at it all night.

Right after the procedure, while I was trying to recover, Gail asked the doctor where the best place in the world was to get treated for multiple myeloma—a cancer we had never heard of before. Dr. Braunstein said, "Little Rock, Arkansas." By the time we had the meeting on Thursday with both my doctors for the definitive diagnosis, I was set to fly to Arkansas the next Tuesday, July 5.

ON TO LITTLE ROCK

At the University of Arkansas for Medical Sciences, there is the ACRC—the Arkansas Cancer Research Center. Sam Walton donated money to the reseach center to start the MIRT—Myeloma Institute for Research and Therapy. He died of multiple myeloma, a rare blood cancer which is still incurable but treatable, especially if caught early.

After getting on the Internet for hours on end, Gail had found information about the myeloma center and an e-mail address for a Dr. Anaissee. She was quite surprised to hear back from him in a matter of hours, and then to receive a telephone call from Dr. Bart Barlogie at 6 p.m. that night. He is the ultimate authority and researcher on myltiple myeloma. People go to Little Rock from all over the world to be treated, and he treats many patients whom other doctors might have given up on. He said he would like for me to come the next day, except it was the 4th of July weekend, so we waited until the fifth.

John Williams, the founder of Post Properties and another friend from childhood, insisted he fly us out to Little Rock on his private jet. With the shock of the cancer diagnosis and the pain from the back fracture, it was a godsend not having to go through the Atlanta airport. We flew out on Tuesday morning after spending 4th of July weekend with friends in Highlands. I didn't want anyone to know about my condition yet, so you can imagine what a strained time it was with all my buddies playing golf while I watched.

I never had any idea how many tests could be done on a body or the amount of blood drawn. I got the first of many catheters in my chest, with three lines called lumens hanging out. At least it stopped most of the needle sticks, which I can't stand. By Thursday, I had started chemotherapy through one of the lumens going into my vein. It was the beginning of what would be more than 1,200 hours of treatment over the next two years.

There are always clinical trials going on at research centers, and getting into one of those frequently holds the most promise for successful treatment. I was enrolled in "Total Therapy II" and began a regimen of chemo and tandem stem cell transplants. I was randomly selected to take the drug thalidomide along with my other drugs. Dr. Barlogie was the first doctor to use thalidomide, which had caused birth defects in the 1950s, for the treatment of multiple myeloma. It cuts off blood circulation to tumors, just like it cut off blood flow to the appendages of a newly forming fetus. The side effects are unpleasant, to say the least. You get neuropathy in your extremities, losing feeling in your fingertips, toes, lips and feet. I had out-of-body experiences, sometimes not knowing where I was. I would lose my balance. I got bloated.

My doctor in Atlanta, Ken Braunstein, told Gail to get me a dozen fresh Krispy Kreme doughnuts every day so I wouldn't lose too much weight. Quite the opposite happened. The steroids and thalidomide I was taking along with the chemo caused me to gain weight. My friends thought I looked like the Pillsbury Doughboy. Gail wouldn't have gotten me those doughnuts anyway.

BACK IN ATLANTA

After a week in Arkansas, we returned to Atlanta overloaded with information and a chemo bottle in my pocket for my first treatment. Little did I know what was to happen over the next months. I made up my mind to beat this insidious disease, no matter what it took. I told my family, "Don't tell me what the statistics are. They don't apply to me." Just because the average life expectancy with myeloma is six to 18 months, "I'm a fighter and a survivor" is my motto.

After my first chemo infusion, which was an easy one, I was admitted to St. Joseph's for my second four-day round. I developed a staph infection, and decided to take the rest at home. I got hooked up to pumps with big bags every four weeks. These would last four days at a time, with Gail switching out the bags every 24 hours and also the batteries which invariably began beeping in the middle of the night. The doctors probably wouldn't have approved of the two Cavalier King Charles spaniels, one half-breed Chihuahua and a large Persian cat in bed with us.

Sometimes, I even felt well enough to take the chemo and pumps and go to the office. I'd make calls and try to work for a few hours before exhaustion set in. All this chemo was in preparation for my first transplant.

COLLECTION AND TRANSPLANT

The purpose of a stem cell transplant is so that a person can get "high dose" chemo. After getting high dose chemo to kill the bone marrow, you have to get back those stored stem cells to kick start your cell blood production. I started the harvest of my stem cells in the fall of '99. You go through a process called aphereses every day until enough cells are collected—hopefully enough for several transplants, or around 20 million. They are then stored in a special nitrogen freezer vault for the future.

Fortunately, my body produced the needed cells and, after more chemo at home, I got my first stem cell transplant. Not until years later was it discovered that my cells were defective.

In late November, Gail and I checked into the Marriott Residence Inn in Little Rock for a month of outpatient treatment. Dr. Barlogie likes to do transplants outpatient if the patient is in good shape, because of the usual problems associated with long hospital stays. Every day, I had to get dressed and go to the chemo room for blood work and tests. I was hairless, bloated and weak. I had to wear a big blue mask if I left the room.

One day, Gail went down first to get the car ready and warmed up, since it was really cold outside. I went down the hall to the elevator, getting weaker with every step. When I got on, I realized I couldn't stand up any more. Too tired to push the button, I just sat down in the corner and fell asleep. Some surprised woman soon got on the elevator on another floor, and asked if I was OK. I told her, "Yes, just a little tired." She got off very quickly.

I'LL BE HOME FOR CHRISTMAS

My friend, Richard Harrell, Mister Georgia Bulldog, sent his company plane out to Little Rock on the 21st of December to take me home for Christmas.

Everybody was happy I was coming home, and I had tears of joy.

My son-in-law, Pano Karatassos, had brought a huge standing rib roast for dinner along with Yorkshire pudding and vegetables—my favorite. He said it would be another 30 minutes, so I decided to lie down for a little while. Next thing I knew it was two a.m., and I had missed the meal.

It was still a wonderful Christmas. All the family felt that the worst of the treatment was over, just one more transplant and some more chemo. The main thing was to get my strength back, surrounded by my loved ones.

Eight

O'LEARY'S RETURN
AND RISE AND FALL

AN UNPRECEDENTED,
BUT NECESSARY, CHANGE

After two 5-6 seasons, Homer had started to have doubts about the effectiveness of the program under Bill Lewis. I don't think it was so much Bill as it was his staff. When the 1994 season started so badly, Homer had some people doing evaluations for him. They came back and said that while it was unprecedented in Tech's history, for the sake of the program they needed to go ahead and make a change. They said to make it *during* the season, rather than the end of the year, in order to give the new coach every opportunity to have a good recruiting year.

Typically, colleges wait until after the last game (which is usually around the first of December) to fire a coach, and then spend 30-45 days to find a new coach.

By that time, the recruiting season is over. In this case, Homer let Bill go after the eighth game, a 41-10 loss to Florida State.

That season was terrible. Not only was there low morale and not much confidence in the coaching staff, there was also strife over the quarterback situation with Donnie Davis and Tommy Luginbill and great polarization among the players. There was no unity on that team. As the defeats started piling up, you could see the deterioration of the program and how difficult things had become for everyone.

Tech people were very upset. Homer went ahead and made the change, with the idea that he would do a more formal search and appoint a permanent head coach after the season.

George O'Leary initially came in with the same discipline he'd had with Ross and Ralph. I think he was really shocked at how far the program had come off track, in terms of discipline, motivation and quality of athletes. He was not impressed with the coaching staff or recruiting, and thought there was a huge drop off.

GEORGE, COME ON UP

For the last three games of the season, O'Leary was named interim head coach. He lost them, and Tech finished 1-10. It still irritates me when I see O'Leary's record and it includes those three losses. However, that was a turning point.

It was obvious to me and several others that George would be the ideal man to become the head coach. One of the things that impressed me about George, that Bobby Ross preached, was the mental toughness he brought and instilled in his players. I've often said great teams are not necessarily the most gifted and the most physically dominating. Great teams are mentally dominating; they know how to win late in the game. They have that confidence and that faith. That's what George taught and what made him so strong.

It wasn't difficult for Homer to realize that George should be the permanent head coach. He was hired soon after the last game.

O'Leary, Really

In 1995, George's first full season as head coach, Tech had a mediocre year. He went 6-5 and lost a real close game to Georgia, 18-17. That first year, as with any new coach, there was a change in culture for the players. They had gone from a pretty loose disciplinary system to a Marine boot camp under George. It was a shock. It took a year or two of recruiting to get the kind of players he wanted.

The first two years, Tech went 6-5 and 5-6, but no one was really concerned about whether George was going to be a good head coach. He operated in many ways like Bobby Ross did. He wasn't much for being involved in public relations. At the same time, George had a unique personality. As George started winning, the fans and alumni saw beyond his "all-business" approach and saw him as the great coach he was.

That first year, George did not have Ralph. He was still with the Chargers. Pat Watson, who's since passed away from a heart attack suffered while he was coaching at Georgia, was George's offensive coordinator and offensive line coach. He stuck to the basics. He believed in running the ball, as most coaches do. Most people don't realize this. It was what Ralph believed in. All the great offensive coaches tell you this: "Yeah, you've got to throw the ball, but if you can't run it, you can't win."

They couldn't make big plays when they had to. I remember Ralph told me, "The secret to offense is you've got to have players who can make big plays. And, most important, you've got to have players who want to make big plays. You teach 'em to *want* to make plays, and that's when you've got a good offense."

Unfortunately, Tech didn't have that, and struggled. At the end of George's first full year, he went to Pat and said, "I'm going to move you back to offensive line coach. I'm going to bring Ralph back. He's my best friend and he's coming back." Slowly, George turned the program back around.

He and Ralph had it going pretty good. They recruited good players, and they had a tough system. Their players started believing in themselves, and they started winning close games.

So there were George and Ralph and their teams, looking for ways to pull it out and win. It all goes back to that mental toughness they had.

*George O'Leary got Tech bowling again, winning the 1997
Carquest Bowl.*

DISCIPLINE

Another thing George did that's essential at Georgia Tech is he maintained strict discipline with his players and their academics. He got a report every day on who went to class, who didn't, who showed up for tutoring, who goofed off in tutoring, who was making good grades and who missed a test. He'd have that report, and he'd work those players one on one.

George told me, "At Georgia Tech, I spend 80 percent of my time not coaching football, but handling these players with their discipline and making sure that their academics get done. We've got to force some of them to go to class and to tutoring sessions. But if you don't do that at Tech, you're going to lose players."

BACK IN THE BOWL BUSINESS

In 1997, George went 7-5. Tech had very good linebackers in Keith Brooking and Ron Rogers, and beat West Virginia 35-30 in the Carquest Bowl. In 1998, Joe Hamilton had finally come into his own under Ralph, and Tech had a great year: 10-2, tied for the ACC championship, finally beat Georgia 21-19 on a last-second field goal and then Notre Dame 35-28 in the Gator Bowl.

Tech football was really coming back, and that bowl game was the crown in the season because it was Notre Dame. We beat them late in the game and did it with defense. Notre Dame was trying to mount a late drive,

Little Joe Hamilton was Tech's B.M.O.C.

and the defense shut them down. It was a huge win for the program and really capped things off for George.

'99 SHOOTOUTS

The next year, 1999, Tech went 8-4, and Joe Hamilton had that great shootout in Tallahassee; however, FSU won 41-35. There was also the overtime shootout with Georgia when a fumble that really wasn't a fumble was called on Jasper Sanks. It stopped a late drive on the goal line.

As much as I'd like to say it as a Tech man, after looking at the play on film from five different angles, probably 20 or 30 times, it was obvious the official didn't see it. However, he made the right call because he didn't see Sanks's knee down. When an official doesn't see it and doesn't blow his whistle, the play's still alive. The next thing you knew, there was Chris Young with the ball.

So while it wasn't a fumble, it *was,* because the official didn't see it. It was just one of those quirky things where Tech got a huge, huge break in the ballgame. Jim Donnan could have kicked a field goal but chose not to. I think Georgia's South Carolina game that year, and that Tech game, probably sealed Donnan's fate.

Earlier, Tech went way ahead and was blowing out Georgia in the third quarter. The game was really getting out of hand. All of a sudden, Quincy Carter, put together these miracle drives, made some great plays and brought Georgia back. Then they got the fumble at the goal line. In overtime, Quincy made a terrible decision

George Godsey was a heady, surprising, top-notch quarterback.

and a bad throw. He underthrew into coverage, and it was intercepted by Marvious Hester.

It was third down on Tech's possession, and O'Leary was being smart. He was going to try a field goal. I was thinking, "You run one more play, don't do anything fancy, maybe run off tackle and get another four, five yards closer." He called for a field goal, and it was blocked.

What happened next showed me the brilliance of George Godsey; it really convinced me the guy was a winner. Godsey had the presence of mind to recover the ball behind the line of scrimmage and return it to the Georgia 21. Then it was fourth down, and Luke Manget kicked a field goal to win it 51-48. To me, that was such a heady play; it set the table for Godsey and his emergence as one of the most surprising quarterbacks I've ever seen play at Georgia Tech.

I didn't think George had an arm or was quick enough, and I didn't think he had the command and presence to be a good quarterback.

Nevertheless, he turned out to be one of the top quarterbacks Tech has ever had. He was so smart, and made such quick reads and quick decisions.

It was one of the most exciting football games, and the most exciting Tech-Georgia game, I've ever seen. It was incredible to watch both teams score that many points [99, the most in series history], and to see the offenses going up and down the field. Neither one could be stopped.

The New Millennium

Everyone assumed that following the 1999 season, 2000 would be a huge letdown after losing Joe Hamilton. They figured that Tech would struggle. Yet they went 9-3 and lost to LSU in the Peach Bowl, in a game a lot of people thought Tech should win. Tech was winning at the half but LSU came back. Godsey hurt his knee, and LSU dominated the second half.

A Farewell to Ralph

Before that game, Ralph left to take the Maryland job. It hurt a tremendous amount because Ralph was the soul of the offense. The players did not take to Ralph on the field, and he didn't spend that much time with them off the field. He wasn't a warm and fuzzy guy from the players' standpoint. However, they all respected him.

This is the difference between coaches who are successful and those who aren't. It's not about having all the players like you that makes the difference in winning or losing. It's whether they *respect* you. The players did respect Ralph, just as they did George.

Ralph was such a stickler for technique, effort and big plays. He wanted guys who came out on the field and said, "Get me the ball," if it was third and eight and the game was on the line. He wanted guys who *wanted* to make plays, such as Joe Hamilton, Kerry Watkins, Dez White, Joe Burns, Charlie Rogers and Kelly Campbell.

If you look at Ralph's Maryland teams, they were all built the same way.

2001, A TECH ODYSSEY

People predicted 2001 would be a big year for Tech football, but they went 8-5. It wasn't a total loss, but it wasn't the year everybody expected. It was the season that people thought Tech would be back in the national championship hunt again.

They had some close games, overtime losses to Clemson and Maryland and a last-minute loss at Virginia. It was a good football team. They were solid, and with some breaks they could've been much better than 8-5. Tech started out 3-0. After routing Navy 70-7, they were scheduled to play at Florida State. The Tuesday following the Navy game was September 11.

The FSU game was postponed until December 1. Tech didn't play for three weeks, then they lost at home to Clemson.

LOSING LATE TO FSU

Many people felt that this was the year Tech might finally beat Florida State. We wanted to play FSU early in the season. People thought that if the game had been played as scheduled, Tech would have been the favorite.

If you watch Florida State, like Miami, they seem to make a lot of mistakes early on and are not as disciplined and focused. As the season goes on, lots of your players start to get nicked up and injured. Most teams don't have the quality depth to back them up.

Florida State was two or three deep at every position. There was not much difference between the starting outside linebacker and the third-team outside linebacker. They could all run, were all big, tough and very fast.

Tech lost to FSU 28-17, and then ended up going to the Seattle Bowl and playing Stanford. By then, George had left for Notre Dame.

SOUTH BEND BOUND?

I'd actually heard rumors from some Tech friends down in Florida. Ash Verlander, a great Tech guy in Jacksonville and a very close friend of Coach Dodd's, was always on top of things and always knew what was happening. One night late in the season he asked me, "Have you heard about Notre Dame making a run at our coach?"

I said, "I've heard all the rumors. I know for an Irishman Notre Dame has that appeal, but I just can't imagine that there's been any contact."

Ash called me about every week or so and said, "I'm telling you, old buddy, there's a friend of mine who's on the board at Notre Dame and he's telling me Notre Dame, indirectly through some alums in Atlanta, has approached O'Leary. And he's the next coach, 'cause Bob Davie's gone." I said, "I'd be shocked at that."

I had talked to George about almost every coach who had been at Tech. I've seen coaches come and go, too many of them. There had been too much turnover since Bobby Dodd. Over the years, I would talk to coaches and say, "This coach left and look what happened. He thought the grass was greener." Georgia Tech may be a hard place to win because it's an academically challenging school. People get tired of hearing that and think Tech is making excuses. It is a fact, though. Tech has rigorous academic requirements, and the players are not exempt from them.

The difficulties are great at Tech, but it is still a great school to coach at. Tech is in a great city, and its alums want to win. They do get mad when Tech doesn't win, but they are not going to run you out of town on a rail if you don't go 11-0 and win the national championship.

THE LURE OF THE IRISH

I thought that the pressure at Notre Dame was intense. It just didn't seem like a good fit for a man like George, specifically because he was not given to meeting the alums, talking about good old Notre Dame or being in front of the national press. I just didn't see a fit there.

I was wrong, however, because of the obvious appeal of Notre Dame, and all it means to many coaches. It is one of the great jobs in the country.

I was shocked when George's agent, Jack Reale, called to tell me he'd accepted a deal with Notre Dame.

I tried to call George a few times, but I couldn't get through to him.

He'd already gone up to Chicago and South Bend. Some of his assistants went with him. Several of them turned him down and did not go.

"Resume-gate"

The big shock came a week later, when "Resume-gate" occurred. George was fired for inaccuracies on his coaching resume after taking the Notre Dame job. It was a total tragedy. Such a simple thing, but at the same time it went to the core.

When this situation exploded, I was as shocked as anyone. I tried to call George for days and finally found out that he was at his lake house. I could only get through to his son. George didn't re-emerge publicly for four or five months. When he did, Mike Tice, who'd played for George in high school, hired him with the Vikings.

He was in a different league now, one that was a little bit more forgiving. It was a fresh start up north, out of this area. While I don't think George was truly happy in terms of his job, he was glad to get a new start under those circumstances.

George and I began to talk again, and soon the old George came out. We talked on the phone, and one time I played a little golf with him at Reynolds Plantation, at his invitation. We still stay in touch. He told me that while he was appreciative of the opportunity, he really preferred the college game over the pros.

It was high times for the Jackets in the 2001 Seattle Bowl.

ON TO ORLANDO

George took the Central Florida job [in 2004], and I believe very strongly that he'll build it into a good football program. It might take him three to five years, but he'll do it.

He's got the diversity of academic majors with a broad-based appeal to players. He is in a great climate and environment. Central Florida is a large school that is growing fast; it's now the second-largest university in Florida.

His athletic director, Steve Orsini, who was at Tech, really supports George and believes in him. They are building new athletic facilities, and I know this man can recruit tough football players to play for him.

SEATTLE

For the Seattle Bowl, Mac McWhorter was named the interim coach. The players loved him. The way they responded to Mac gave me a feeling that we were going to win that game even before we flew out to Seattle. The attitude, the spirit, the player support for Mac was very obvious. I was told they had a lot of players-only meetings where they said, "We've got to win this game not for ourselves, but for Mac McWhorter if we want him to be our next head coach." Even the seniors stood up and said so.

I think that was the best-played game Tech had that year in terms of effort, enthusiasm and attitude. They really wanted to win, and they focused, played hard and beat a pretty good Stanford team 24-14.

I remember that reverse down at the goal line that Kelly Campbell scored on to clinch it. What a great call! Billy O'Brien made that call. Afterward, I asked him, "Why didn't you do that more during the year?" He replied, "Well, we ran more of a conservative style of offense. But in this game Mac said, 'Open the door, let it all out, call it the way you feel it.'" Mac let the coaches coach, and the players play—and they all responded.

Nine

CHAN GAILEY

CHAN'S THE MAN

After the final game of the 2001 season, all the players and coaches were excited about the win, but moreso about the possibility that Mac McWhorter might be the new head coach. But athletic director Dave Braine and the athletic board went through an exhaustive process to interview a lot of candidates. So it was a surprise the next week when Chan Gailey was introduced as the new head coach.

While I knew of Chan, i'd never really met him. I was very impressed when I had a chance to spend some time with him. I think Chan went through a pretty good adjustment from the pro game to the college game, particularly his first year. But he made some personal adjustments and had a surprisingly good year in 2003, even though he lost 12 players because of academics.

I think that situation convinced Chan that his focus had to be on football but also the academic standing of his players. He realized how important academics are at Georgia Tech.

For Openers, Tony Hollings

Chan's first season, 2002, was pretty successful for a new coach.

His team went 7-6 and won a couple of big games. They also struggled late in the year.

Tony Hollings had been moved from defense, where he was an overlooked player, to running back in the spring of 2002. He'd asked to move because they didn't have any running backs. Joe Burns was gone, and Tony volunteered. He was an unbelievable surprise.

Not only did he have speed and quickness, he had that great instinct to find daylight. Many runners lower their head and don't look downfield to where the open field is. The great backs have that vision and presence. Hollings had that.

He was leading the nation in rushing and scoring when he injured his knee late in the Brigham Young game, the fourth game of the year, and he was out for the season.

Without Hollings, Tech struggled and won four of its last nine games.

Tech was trounced by Georgia 51-7 in Athens and went to the Silicon Valley bowl game to play Fresno State, which upset Tech 30-21. The field was in bad shape, just terrible. They had workers coming out during the game and throwing sand on the field because it was so sloppy and in such bad condition.

Tech played terribly, which left a bad taste in everybody's mouth—players, coaches, fans, everybody.

A BAD SPRING

The next spring was when the academic casualties hit, and it really upset the Tech community. In many ways, it was a lack of focus by the tutoring personnel at Tech. Many people thought it could've been avoided.

In Chan's defense, he wasn't charged with that academic responsibility, but he's learned he has to make academics a primary focus [in order] to be successful at Tech.

The 2003 season looked pretty gloomy, with Tony Hollings and defensive end Tony Hargrove academically ineligible. Yet that team finished 7-6 and won a big bowl game against Tulsa in the Humanitarian Bowl, 52-10.

A TOUGH START, BUT THEN...

The 2003 opener was at Brigham Young. With a freshman quarterback, as anticipated, it was difficult to win on the road. Tech lost 24-13.

But the next week, in the home opener, Tech upset a highly touted Auburn team 17-3. Reggie Ball was fantastic.

That day they opened up the new North Stands upper deck, and the redone East Stands. It was a big occasion, and Tech totally dominated Auburn, both defensively and offensively. It really excited Tech fans because Auburn, up until the late '80s, had always been a traditional rival.

There were some great Tech-Auburn games. In fact, many people would love to see that rivalry continue on a regular basis, because of the excitement it always brought to both Tech and Auburn.

ANOTHER TALLAHASSEE HEARTBREAK

The following week, Tech lost a heartbreaker at Florida State, a last-minute 14-13 loss. Tech had dominated the game throughout and was leading 13-0 until Florida State scored twice in the last seven minutes. The second touchdown came with just under two minutes left.

It was almost like Tech ran out of gas. It was a warm night and, with Tech playing without a lot of depth, it looked like late in the game they just lost that edge. FSU came on and scored to really win a game it should've lost. That would've been a huge win, the first time Tech had beaten Florida State since FSU joined the ACC.

A CLEMSON COLLAPSE

The next week was a total blowout by Clemson, 37–3, and probably one of the most disappointing losses I've ever seen Tech suffer. Many people thought Tech would win that game, playing at home and coming off such strong showings against Auburn and Florida State.

But Clemson was sharp, especially quarterback Charlie Whitehurst, who threw for three touchdowns in the second quarter. Tech was flat and didn't play with a lot of emotion. The result was an embarrassment for Tech.

UP AGAIN...

Tech went on the road and beat Vanderbilt in overtime 24–17, and then came home and beat a pretty good N.C. State team with quarterback Philip Rivers. Rivers never seemed to get in sync thanks to the different blitzes and blitz packages that Jon Tenuta, Tech's defensive coordinator, threw at him.

It was like N.C. State had no clue what was coming at them, and Rivers really was frustrated. Tech has beaten N.C. State three straight years, and eight of the last nine.

Tech played great defensively to beat Wake Forest and Maryland in a Thursday night game, and was 5-3 with a four-game winning streak.

...THEN A DUKE DEBACLE

Then shockingly, Duke, which had lost a record 30 ACC games in a row, not only upset Tech at Durham but trounced them 41-17. It was a game where Duke played with tremendous emotion and Tech was totally flat.

But Tech teams have usually not played well at Durham. Going back to my experience as a player, I always remember Wallace Wade Stadium as being an uninspiring place to play. It's not a big crowd, and the field is sort of wedged in. There's not a lot of sideline room. As a former player now watching games up there, Tech teams have not played with a lot of emotion and inspiration. It's just one of those quirks.

They've won up there, but they haven't won impressively. This game got out of hand, Duke poured it on in the second half, and Tech never really got on track.

Duke was playing for something else that day, too: Ted Roof, the interim head coach, was a great player at Tech, had coached under O'Leary and had wanted to stay at Tech. But Chan, being a new coach, wanted to bring his staff and coordinators in. The combination of all of those factors really inspired Ted and, in turn, he really got his team fired up to play.

They were playing to help him get the job on a permanent basis. I remember Ted was interviewed on the field right after the game, and he gave out his home address and invited anyone listening and all Duke fans to come to his house for a postgame party. It must have been some party. After Duke beat North Carolina to finish the season, Ted got the job.

UP YET AGAIN...

The next week, Tech finally put North Carolina away in the second half with the running game and won 41-24.

That game was frustrating; in the first half, the run was there but it seemed like Tech was trying to mix in a lot more passes. In the second half, they just started pounding the ball inside, and North Carolina couldn't stop the running game. Tech finally took control and ran away with it. P.J. Daniels rushed for 240 yards, including 155 in the second half, and Jonathan Smith caught a touchdown pass, passed for a TD and scored another on a long punt return.

THEN AGAIN...

The Virginia game in Charlottesville is another one of those games that Tech has great difficulty winning. Tech has not won in Charlottesville since 1990, that great game when Virginia was No. 1.

There's that jinx, and this time Virginia pulled away as the game went on and really dominated late in the game. Matt Schaub was fantastic throwing the ball, and we just couldn't make a big play late in the game to get back in it. Virginia won for the sixth straight time in Charlottesville 29-17.

On the Saturday after Thanksgiving, Georgia jumped out 14-0 in the first quarter and it seemed Tech was always trying to play catch-up. That's very difficult

In bitterly cold Boise, Chan Gailey's (right) second season ended with a warm feeling.

because Georgia had a great defense. You typically don't play catch-up against Georgia.

David Greene had a big game as well. In my view, he was the difference in that game. He made big plays and he didn't make mistakes. Reggie Ball was playing in his first Tech-Georgia game as a true freshman. Regardless of what people say, that game is different.

There's a lot of pressure on you. Having played quarterback in those games, I know what that means.

It was pretty obvious to me that it was a rough day for Reggie. They rattled him. He'll respond better now that he's had a year under his belt.

A GOOD ENDING

In Boise, the blowout of Tulsa in the Humanitarian Bowl was unbelievable. To beat them as badly as we did, it was just total domination.

They took out P.J. Daniels early in the fourth quarter, or he could probably have gained another, well, who knows? He might have rushed for 400 yards. But Chan wasn't going to leave him in just to do that. Still, it was a great way to end the season.

I believe the 2004 season will be an even better year for Tech, even though the schedule's tougher with the addition of Miami and Virginia Tech, now in the ACC. Chan's system will be in place for the third year, which usually is a pivotal year for a head coach. That's when he has a chance for his recruits to play, for his system to be honed, and for players, coaches and fans to understand the system better.

Plus, Reggie Ball, who was a true freshman in 2003 and had a phenomenal year as the ACC Rookie of the Year, is back and should be more mature and seasoned.

Ten

AL CIRALDO

AL

As a high school junior, I remember Al Ciraldo doing Georgia Tech basketball games when Roger Kaiser was the big Tech star. I heard all of the great Ciraldo-isms:

"Gtt!" for "Good."

"He missed a bunny!" for a missed layup.

"Toe meets leather!" for the kickoff in football.

"Brothers and sisters, we've got a barnburner brewing today!"

I think that's what it was: "A barnburner brewing today." But I never figured that out.

In high school, I used to listen to Tech basketball games when Roger Kaiser and Dave Denton played. Bobby Dews and Josh Powell. To hear Al describe those players: It wasn't "Roger." It was "Rajah!" R-A-J-A-H. "Rajah Kaiser, for two...Gtt!"

Little Bobby Dews, [who became] a coach with the Atlanta Braves, and Dave "The Duke" Denton, behind his back. He was the first college basketball player I'd ever seen dribble behind his back. For that day and time, Dave Denton was a very flamboyant and exciting basketball player.

I heard Al do those games on radio, and it was just one of those nail biting experiences to listen to Georgia Tech basketball and hear him describe it. I never will forget the Tech-Georgia game at old Woodruff Hall in Athens. It was either Kaiser's junior or senior year, and a very close game. I'll always remember Al saying something about Woodruff Hall was in such bad disrepair, and the roof leaked, and it was the only basketball arena in the Southeast where weather could play a factor in the outcome of the game.

Kaiser hit a remarkable shot late in the game, and Al went into one of those screaming fits: "Rajah! Rajah Kaiser hits for two! Gtt! And this game goes into overtime! Heeeeyyyy, Rajah Kaiser!"

ALL THAT EMOTION

All of Al's exaggeration and the emotion he put into it really made it fun to listen to, but also nerve-wracking. You almost felt like you were out there playing, which is what I loved about his delivery. He could make a five-yard loss sound like a 50-yard gain.

It would be a description like this: "Danny Myers sets his charges. Barks signals...Hands off to Eddie Lee Ivery...Eddie Lee, off the left side! Eddie Lee, breaking out to the side...He's cut back. He's coming back to the center of the field...He heads upfield and he's tackled for a five-yard loss! Hey, Kim King, this Eddie Lee Ivery can really turn a big play!"

Al was always good at making things exciting, even when they were very boring games. I can remember many, many times when Tech would be on the right end of a very lopsided win, and yet Al was still making it sounded as if it was Notre Dame in the last second down on the goal line. He had a knack for putting excitement into a broadcast. Al could get you fired up during the pregame show. He just had that emotional ability to really get into a game. If you were a Tech fan listening, you could really get excited.

HANG ON, AL!

I'll never forget the first game with Al that really stuck out to me.

Tech played at Tennessee in 1977. I'd started doing the games in 1974. We had the old microphones that had the wire set hanging around your neck. The microphone would literally hang loose on your chest.

If you just turned your head, you couldn't speak into the microphone, so you always had to be careful and turn with the microphone.

They had those long black cords, and the engineer, sort of like a team of horses, had to pull the wires to make sure that when you turned you didn't get all tangled up. Tennessee has a very large and steep stadium.

Al got so excited when we scored a touchdown that he literally stood up and turned, and it was almost like he was talking to people in the booth. And he lost his balance. Somehow, the wire got wrapped around Al's neck and he was leaning over the outside of the booth. One of the spotters grabbed Al by the back of his belt to keep him from falling out of the booth with all that wire hanging around him.

But Al, being the professional that he was, never missed a beat. He just kept right on going through all that. He kept making the call.

It just amazed me how excited and enthusiastic he could be.

ANOTHER CALL...

We were playing at Memphis State in 1980, Bill Curry's first year. On one play, Mike Kelley, the quarterback, faked it to the fullback, Ronny Cone, and threw a play-action pass to the flanker, Jeff Keisler, who made the catch and proceeded to go down the sideline. But Al never saw the pass.

All he saw was the inside fake, and he thought that was the handoff. Cone was hit, but being the good player he was, Cone was faking that he had the ball and was fighting and churning in there. And Al's describing the action:

"Cone gets the handoff from Kelley, and he SMACKS into the middle of the line! And he's hit, and he's spun! And he's fighting and clawing!"

Now, everybody's cheering because here's our flanker, Keisler, running free down the sideline. He's going for a touchdown. Finally, he gets knocked out of bounds around the the three.

Al never missed a beat, even though he didn't pick it up until the play was over. He said, "And Keisler is KNOCKED out of bounds at the three-yard line! First and goal! Great run, Kim King!" I just said, "Right you are, Al." I was just shaking my head and smiling.

HEY, KIM KING!

I remember the Citadel game in 1987, Bobby Ross's first game at Tech. We beat the Citadel 51-12, and it was one of those yawners. The Citadel was clearly overmatched.

Late in the game, Tech had put the third string in and was still moving the ball. Tech had a tight end named Alonzo Watson. He was from Forsyth, Georgia, and he was a computer science major. With only a minute or two left, Tech had its third-team quarterback in and he threw a pass to Watson, who caught it and ran for another 25 yards before he was tackled at about the 10.

You would have thought that was a play that won the Super Bowl, to hear Al describe it. He got so excited. I was almost asleep from boredom and certainly not into the broadcast, so I wasn't adding anything to it. Yet Al, with this total energy and total Ciraldo delivery, was so excited.

He said, "Watson catches the ball! And he's finally tackled at the 10! Hey, Kim King, this Alonzo Watson from Forsyth, Georgia, he's a computer science major and Kim, this kid can compute!"

I gave my usual reply: "Right you are, Al. He can compute."

EARLY ON...

In one of my first years doing the games, Tech had an offensive tackle named Jeff Urczyk. After the game, we were down in the old locker room under the East Stands. It was really in bad shape. The ceiling tiles were hanging down and there were water stains all over the baseboards. Things were mildewed and moldy. Every now and then you'd see a little mouse or rat scrambling around.

They put us in this little storage room that was literally about four feet wide and had a very low ceiling, about five and a half feet high. We were on little stools in there, talking to players after the game. Jeff Urczyk, who was from up north and didn't have a lot of time for people, was in a nasty mood even though he'd played very well.

It was really hot in this little room, and sweaty, and Jeff was tired and soaking wet. I was starting to sweat and Al was soaking wet.

Finally, when we came back from a commercial, I could tell Urczyk was a little irritated that we were keeping him there from taking a shower.

Al turned to him and said, "Great game today, Jeff Urczyk, big tackle from Pennsylvania. Jeff...why Georgia Tech?" In other words, why did you pick Georgia Tech? Urczyk was very irritated at the question.

Rather than give Al a standard reply, he looked up at the ceiling at these tiles hanging down and water dripping and said, "Al, it was the facilities."

And Al said, "Great facilities here at Tech, Jeff Urczyk." I thought I would die. I was biting my lip, trying to keep from laughing. I'll never forget that.

A START

When I was in high school, Al wasn't calling Tech football games. It was Jack Hurst and Bob Fulton. When I played at Tech, Al moved up to the color. Milo Hamilton, who'd replaced Jack Hurst doing play by play, left in '74 and that's when Ciraldo moved up to play by play.

Tech still owned the radio station then—WGST— and Coach Dodd moved Al up to do play-by-play. Then he called me to do the color. I never put my name in the hat, and really didn't know anything about it. Coach Dodd called one day and he was always real to the point:

"Kimmy? Milo's left us. He's gone. I'm gonna make Al the play-by-play man, and I want you to do color. Will you do it for me?"

I said, "Coach, I'll do it for you, but I've never had any training. I don't have a radio voice." He said, "But you understand football. You just keep your mouth shut.

Don't you say a lot. You understand? You do those games for me." BAM! It wasn't like I could say no, or let me think about it. It was already a done deal.

Al's Sense of Style

Al was exciting to work with, and a guy who never said anything bad about anybody. That's what I remember most about him.

After the second or third year, I got a call from the station manager at WGST. He said, "I'm tired of going to the games and seeing you guys wear different clothes." What he was really saying was Al was still wearing those 1940 suits he had. Al was not too extravagant with money, particularly when it came to personal comfort things.

The station manager said, "I'm gonna get y'all a pair of slacks, any color you want, but I want you all to have the same blazer. I've got it set up on a trade deal with Muse's. I want you to take Al down there and make sure he gets that blazer and a nice pair of slacks, just like you."

I said, "Great." I picked Al up and we went to Muse's, when it was downtown, and a salesman was waiting for us. Al said, "You go first, brother." He called everybody "brother." I picked out a nice pair of light gray wool slacks and a really nice blue blazer, and they fitted me.

Then it was Al's turn. Al turned to the salesman and said, "You know, that coat costs about $400." Back then, that was a pretty good piece of change. The slacks

The young, debonair Al Ciraldo behind the WGST microphone.

were about $90. Al said, "I think I'll just take the cash."
So he got the cash, and didn't buy the clothes.

When the station manager found out about it, he absolutely blew up.

He came to the next game. Here I am, in my blazer and slacks and Al's still there in with a wide lapel, double-breasted 1940's suit. It didn't go over well.

A GREAT SET-UP MAN

Al was great to work with. He always set me up. He'd always say, "Kim King, this is a great defensive performance by Lucius Sanford, he's really played well in this first half."

He always laid it out for me and he never put me out on a limb.

He would let me give my opinions. Out at Air Force, when Eddie Lee Ivery broke the NCAA single-game rushing record, we went out with the team on Friday and it was a beautiful fall day: Maybe 60 degrees, dry air, beautiful sunshine, very few clouds, just a remarkable day.

The next morning I woke up and looked out the hotel window about seven o'clock and it was a blizzard. I took Al to the local Kmart in a cab and I bought us sweatsuits, gloves and hats because we didn't come pre-pared for it.

Before the game, I always have a routine where I go down and look at the field, look at the players warming up. I enjoy doing that and it gives me a feeling for how Tech would stack up talent-wise. Well, it was snowing and the wind was blowing about 25 miles an hour and the snow was coming down sideways. It would sting your eyes.

The field was a sheet of ice. I slid out in the end zone about five yards and then I just slid back. I was afraid I was going to fall down. I went back up to the press box and Al, in his typical style right before the kickoff, said, "Kim King, what kind of game are you looking for today?"

I said, "Al, the first team to kick a field goal is going to win it 3-0. These are just unplayable conditions. Nobody can stand up out there. There's ice on the field, snow's coming down. The quarterback's not going to be able to see down the field. The receivers are not going to be able to pick out the ball. This is going to be a low-scoring game."

Of course, it was a track meet. Tech won 42-21. Eddie Lee ran for 356 yards. Dave Ziebart, the Air Force quarterback, had a huge day and threw for about 350 yards. There was just a tremendous amount of offense.

But Al was always good. He never put me on the spot. I tried to untangle him when he'd mistakenly describe a play, and would always try to gently let him off the hook without saying, "Al, you're wrong." I'd just repeat what happened so that people listening would be able to follow it.

VIRGINIA

The Virginia game in 1990, oh, that was just unbelievable. When Scott Sisson kicked that field goal, Al was hollering and I got a little hollering in, too. I sort of lost control, which I normally didn't do. But that game really excited me. That was a remarkable game, not only for the contest itself. To be there with Al, and let him get emotional as he could do against the weakest opponents, just made that game almost unbearable.

The nerves, the tension, the sweat, Al put all of that into the broadcast, which is why I thought he was such a great broadcaster.

Some people like just the basic facts. Some people like to be inspired, and for emotion to come through. That was Al's style. That game was off the charts for him.

We both were down at halftime because Tech was trailing 28-14, and pretty well getting hammered. Lo and behold, they tied it up, then even went ahead. It seesawed a little bit. Every minute, as it went further and deeper into the game, Al became even more emotional.

At that time, we were in an open booth right there in the middle of the Virginia section. We were taking a lot of abuse. I was aware of it because there was a big guy right in front of us, and he didn't like us one bit. But Al never got fazed by any of that. It was almost like we were in an empty room, nobody was around and we were watching the game on TV. That was the kind of focus Al had; he wouldn't let anyone intimidate or bother him.

When Sisson hit that field goal, Al went into one of the real emotional peaks, even for him: "And Scott Sisson hits the ball...The kick is high, it's long, it's low, it's short...IT'S GOOD!!! Kim King, Scott Sisson, he's kicked a field goal! Georgia Tech has won!   Georgia Tech has won!"

I was screaming, too. We were a pair of fanatics. I think I gave it one of these: "Woo-hoo!" It was just unbelievable. Even after the game when we were in the locker room, Al was so fired up and so emotional, it was just great. I left that game like a kid. I had the emotions of a kid again, I was so excited Tech had knocked off the No. 1 team in the country. The way they did it to win, and to be fired up like Al could fire you up, it was just such an emotional high.

A Mutual Love Affair

Al really loved Georgia Tech. I can think of nobody who had more affection for that school than Al Ciraldo. He really did. He had great devotion and respect for the players and the coaches. He honored Georgia Tech. In turn, Tech honored him by naming the broadcast booth for him. He had a long love affair with Georgia Tech, and was loved by a lot of people.

I miss Al, I really do.

Al (right) and I returned to the sky-high press box and booth at Tennessee in 1979.

MISSING AL

It was a big shock to me the first game we did without Al. It wasn't the same for a while, not having him around.

Bob McCann came on board in '92 as the play-by-play man for a year. I was doing the color and Al did the halftime show and some postgame.

It just wasn't the same without him.

Al enjoyed Tech and Tech enjoyed him. He could motivate and inspire people. You'd go to a basketball game at the Coliseum and before every tip-off the student section would all rise and say, "Hi, Al!" Al would stand up and recognize them. That was an ongoing tradition for Georgia Tech.

Al will be remembered forever. I'll never forget him, because he was that important to me, and I think he was that important to Georgia Tech athletics.

WES

Wes Durham, Al's replacement, is absolutely one of the top broadcasters in the business.

He knows the players, knows the coaches, knows the stats. He can be very professional, and he can put emotion into it when he needs to.

He can be very somber when it's needed, and Wes really understands the game.

I have announced Tech games with Wes since 1995, and I have great resect for him as a broadcaster and, even more importantly, as a spokesman for Georgia Tech sports.

Wes and I have shared some great moments in Tech football history. Some big wins and losses: the "Catch" at Clemson, the "Fumble" against Georgia on the goal line, and the "Kick" in Athens that gave Tech its first victory over Georgia in five years. It was his enthusiasm and professionalism that made all those plays an enduring part of Georgia Tech history.

Wes is a true friend, and my admiration extends beyond the broadcasting booth. He and his wife, Lynn, are the proud parents of fraternal twins, Emily and Will. His children will surely remember, as they mature, coming to the radio booth all dressed up in their Georgia Tech colors.

Eleven

REFLECTIONS

SIDELINED AGAIN

In the winter of 2004, I began having slight symptoms of what was yet to come. Being the energetic, never-slow-down kind of person that I am, I didn't listen to my body. I continued to work long hours, go spring turkey hunting and play golf in all kinds of weather. I would not admit what I knew instinctually—that cancer was back.

In March, I got some Tech fans together, including my good friends Jamie and Harold Reynolds, to go out to San Antonio. The "Techsters" had made it to the NCAA Final Four with their great coach Paul Hewitt, and I planned to be there. Although Tech lost in the final to Connecticut, it was a great feeling to be one of the last two teams in the country still playing. The

Tech support was magic as we swarmed the downtown Riverwalk in our gold and white.

The morning after the game, Gail and I were flying to Little Rock for my usual six-month check-up. The weather in San Antonio prevented us from taking off from the private airport—planes were stacked up to go and we were way down the list. Even though we got special clearance to leave, it was too late in Arkansas for the scheduled testing to be done. Oh well, I thought, "I'll just schedule the tests for a couple of months from now, when I'm not so busy. No big deal." Over the next few weeks, I became lethargic and tired easily.

Our family—three children, two sons-in-law and two grandsons—had a planned trip to our Sea Island beach house in May. No way was I going to miss our family get together because I was low on energy. I spent a lot of time resting in bed and could only play nine holes of golf at a time. It was obvious something was seriously wrong with me, yet we had our best trip ever—one of those special times when everyone gets along well, the weather is perfect, the grandchildren are precious and there is serenity.

On Monday after our return, I knew I was sick. I called Ken Braunstein, who sent me to the lab for blood work. I was too weak to drive to an important meeting that afternoon, so Gail took me and waited in the lobby. Ken called on her cell phone and told her to get me to the hospital and have the family meet us there. At St. Joseph's, with me in the bed in my pajamas, we got the news. Not only was cancer back, this time it was second-ary acute myelogenous leukemia. This blood cancer is aggressive and resistant to treatment.

I called my friend Dr. Bart Barlogie who was in St. Louis at a medical meeting. "Get out to Arkansas immediately," he said. When I told him we would be there in a couple of days, he was adamant. "I mean tonight." So, by 11 p.m. I was in the hospital in Little Rock.

After some trials with experimental drugs failed, I had some very tough chemo treatment and reached remission. "I'm a fighter and I never quit" is still my motto.

Surprise of My Life

One morning about seven weeks into my hospital stay, I had the biggest surprise of my life. Wes Durham showed up in my hospital room, with the news that Georgia Tech was naming the locker room after me. It is the single greatest honor I have ever received, and I was speechless to say the least. Tech has been such an important part of my life for over 50 years. The fact that my name will remain at the school permanently, even after I'm gone, is overwhelming. Certainly, my spirit will always be there as those players get dressed and run out on that field. I will always be there cheering them on in victory and defeat.

Tech Memories from the '60s

Dean George Griffin, "Mr. Georgia Tech", made a presentation every year at the beginning of the football

season. He came to the locker room with a brown paper
"Colonial" grocery bag. The Colonial store was about
the only grocery chain in Atlanta at the time, and of
course, plastic bags hadn't been invented. The bag, as it
turned out, contained a big rock. "Dean," as we called
him, spoke on and on about the possible recipients of
this famous award he was bestowing and its importance.
Only the finest all-around athlete and student would get
this "Sack Brain Award."

Tommy Carlisle was eliminated from consideration
for getting an 80 on a test. After much rigamarole,
"Dean" brought the sack my way, handed it to me, and
announced that I was the winner. My brain was just like
that rock. We never quite figured out the significance

*Gail and I listen to "Mr. Georgia Tech," Dean George Griffin,
speaking at a Georgia Tech Alumni Club function.*

of the whole affair, but always looked forward to seeing which senior each year would get to be president of the Sack Brain Club. I guess my third-team Academic All-America standing helped me.

⌘ ⌘ ⌘

Growing up in Southwest Atlanta, I played all sports from the time I could walk. My older brother Buddy, also a good athlete, would let me play with the bigger boys. It really helped my competitive nature and made me a better athlete to play against those guys. Buddy had crooked teeth, and Mom put braces on him just like everybody else had at the time. He was always getting kicked and hit on his braces and coming home with a bloody mouth. When my time came for braces, I said "no way" to that. My high school coach, Joe O'Malley, a former Georgia football great, often said, "King, it would be an improvement for you to get your teeth knocked out." As it turned out, I did.

I was breaking up one of those inevitable fights at a joint fraternity party after a Tech game, when I got side-swiped and my front teeth sheared off. Dr. Aaron King, who has been my dentist and friend since my playing days, fixed me up with some nice-looking crowns in the front. I still go to him every six months. He has meant so much to the Tech players, and I don't think there's ever been a game when he wasn't on the sidelines. Of course, with players wearing mouthguards these days, he doesn't have as many broken teeth to fix. Aaron has been a truly vital part of the Georgia Tech sports program for over 40 years.

Kim King, the very young lefthanded quarterback for E.L. Connally Elementary School, in action at John A. White Park in 1957.

⌘ ⌘ ⌘

One year when we were playing a tough Auburn team, they were beating us badly. I mean we were getting slapped around. Giles Smith, our starting tailback, came slowly back to the huddle one time with his helmet askew and asked in earnest, "Can't we just go to the Varsity, get a Big Orange and talk about this? It's going to be a long day."

Lew Woodruff, our gruff backfield coach, came up with some hand signals for receivers. He was showing a clenched fist, an open palm by his side and lots of others he had invented for use during a game. That clenched fist signified a hitch pass; when he asked Dennis James what it meant, Dennis who had not been paying attention, said, "The bomb, man, the bomb." We all laughed uproariously.

⌘ ⌘ ⌘

One year when we played a good Duke team, they had a great running back named Jay Calabrese. The plan was for Tommy Carlisle and Eric Wilcox to hit him really hard early on to intimidate him. Carlisle and Wilcox zeroed in on Calabrese from opposite sides. Calabrese ducked and they ran into each other so hard, both were knocked out and had to sit out several plays. So much for the "tough guys" intimidating the other team.

⌘ ⌘ ⌘

In the Georgia game my senior year, the first-down marker chain broke. We were inside the one-yard line with fourth and goal to go. The referee stuck a pencil in the broken link, making the chain longer than the standard 10 yards. We missed the first down by the nose of the football and went on to lose the game. It was the key play. As I fussed with the official, he reminded me that he could call a 15-yard unsportsmanlike penalty if I didn't get off the field. End of argument.

⌘ ⌘ ⌘

My senior year at Tech, I roomed with Eric Wilcox, a junior linebacker and all-around tough guy from Tyler, Texas. At that time all student athletes, except married ones, lived in dormitories. Eric liked to go out on weeknights, not necessarily to the library. When he arrived back at the room, usually around 11 p.m., he was always hungry.

This fella on our hall that we called "Joltin'" Joe Massey from Macon, Georgia was usually Eric's target. He was chosen to make a "V" run. Eric would squirt Ronson lighter fluid under Joe's door, light it with glee and wait for Joe to come running out. In fear for his life, Joe was always willing to walk to the Varsity for chili dogs. By the end of the quarter, poor Joe's door could be unlocked from the outside hall by reaching under the burned lower half. Eric, by the way, still holds the record for most tackles in a single game against Georgia in 1967.

⌘ ⌘ ⌘

During spring break each year, most players made the pilgrimage to Daytona Beach, Florida. One year, Tommy Carlisle, who was a dapper dresser and considered a real ladies man, went down there with a bunch of coeds. Needless to say they weren't Tech coeds, because we didn't have many on campus in the '60s. Coach Dodd was adamant about registering for classes on time and attending those classes regularly. We got away with nothing when it came to school.

Well, when Tommy arrived back in Atlanta on Sunday night before Monday morning registration, he realized he had left his alligator shoes in the motel in Daytona. This was before anyone could afford shoes

Georgia Tech's "Fearsome Threesome:" (L to R) tailback Lenny Snow, Coach Bobby Dodd and quarterback Kim King.

Kim King eludes All-American George Patton (left) and All-SEC nose guard Dickie Phillips (right) during the 1966 Georgia-Georgia Tech game in Athens.

like that. It was getting late at night, but Tommy turned around and drove back to get those shoes. Somehow he made it back in time to register the next morning.

TECH FOREVER

As I reflect on my 50 years of association with Georgia Tech, I am sitting in my Midtown penthouse office. It's a corner office with large windows facing Tech and downtown Atlanta. Growing up, I never thought I would be here. Actually, most people who knew I was trying to develop in this area thought I had no chance of pulling it off. I knew that Georgia Tech needed to expand the campus and going across the expressway was the most logical choice.

I joined efforts with TUFF, The University Financing Foundation, Inc., which includes such outstanding Tech men as John Aderhold, Frank Smith and Tom Hall. With their help and financing, we developed what is known as Cynergy, a mixed-use project. This has become a milestone complex that has kicked off a rebirth of Midtown Atlanta.

I have traveled far and wide, met a lot of successful people, but I've never known any better group than those who made it through the rigors of Georgia Tech. We are a different breed—people who produce, won't take no for an answer and never give up.

I still get a thrill when I hear the "Ramblin Wreck" fight song and will always be proud to be a Yellow Jacket.

Epilogue

When the time came early that Tuesday morning, when "the young left-hander" finally left us, Kim King was at home. By his bedside were the people who loved him most: His wife, Gail, their daughters, Angela and Abby, and son Beau. Six days after turning 59, five years after first falling ill, King died peacefully on October 12, 2004. His wife's 57th birthday.

"He waited until my birthday, and it's the greatest gift he ever gave me because he will no longer suffer," Gail King said of her husband, Bobby Dodd's last and favorite quarterback, a 40-year legendary figure in Georgia Tech athletics and one of Atlanta's foremost commercial real estate developers. King died of secondary acute myelogenous leukemia.

"It was such a blessing for him to be finished with the pain and suffering," said Gail King. "And, it was his way of saying, 'Gail, don't ever forget me,'" she said with a soft, sad chuckle.

For Georgia Tech and Atlanta, Kim King remains unforgettable. The kid from the West End and old Brown High became Tech's starting, record-setting quarterback from 1965-67. For 30 years, he was the radio color analyst for Tech football—"the young lefthander," as the late play-by-play man Al Ciraldo first nicknamed the quarterback he later worked beside for 19 seasons in the booth.

"There are a lot of people who know Kim King only from 30 years of being on the radio, never saw him take a snap, and yet they buy into and understand what he stood for," said Wes Durham, the Tech broadcaster and close friend of King who worked with him from 1995-2003 before King's illness sidelined him.

"Kim embodied the school. This is a serious piece of Georgia Tech legend and lore and history that's gone. It was something you could reach out and talk to, and it was the comforting voice that was there on Saturday."

"He was Mr. Georgia Tech," said then athletics director Dave Braine. "Since 1964, he was involved in more than 300 football games at Georgia Tech—almost a third of the games Tech's played. Nobody else can say that. When you hear the names of Heisman and Alexander and Dodd, and Homer Rice (Tech's distinguished former AD), Kim King's name has to go in there, too."

King's penthouse office at Kim King Associates, Inc. is on the top floor of Centergy, the complex he built adjacent to Tech's Midtown campus at Technology Square. Earlier [in 2004] King was named the state of Georgia's "Most Respected CEO" by *Georgia Trend* magazine.

Bill Curry was a star Tech player when King arrived on The Flats in the fall of 1963. "I have never known anyone like him and do not expect to find another like him in our lifetime," said Curry, who returned to Tech as head coach in 1980. Curry became a close friend of King, recalling his "rare combination of honesty, passion and an indefatigable desire to win."

"It is my firm belief," Curry said, "that had it not been for Kim King in the late '70s and early '80s, we would not have enjoyed a fraction of the success we have experienced in athletics."

King was first named to the school's athletic board in 1974 by then-Tech president Joseph Pettit, who was not an advocate for football. "In the late '70s," Braine recalled, "Kim was responsible, along with Homer Rice, for raising the money for the Edge Athletics Center, which saved Georgia Tech athletics."

King actually wanted Bobby Dodd, his legendary coach, to be the honorary chairman of a fund-raising campaign to build a new athletics center. Dodd declined and told King, who'd chaired the feasibility study for the project, that there was neither administrative nor financial support.

King helped arrange a trip to the White House, where Dodd met President Jimmy Carter, who asked him to help Tech build the athletics complex.

"Yes, Mr. President, I will," said Dodd, who, on the flight home said, "Damn you, Kim King. You weren't man enough to get me to say yes. But I couldn't say no to the president of the United States." The Edge Center opened in 1982.

As a quarterback, King led the Jackets to a Gator Bowl victory as a sophomore and to the Orange Bowl as a junior. Tech won its first nine games in that 1966 season, including a 6-3 win over No. 8 Tennessee, after which King was carried off Grant Field by jubilant Tech students.

He received numerous awards and accolades, including the Tech Athletic Association Total Person Award in 1998, and was later named one of Tech's 50 Greatest Athletes of the 20th Century in 2000.

On the radio, King was usually analytical to Ciraldo's "Hold on, brothers and sisters!"

Yet Wes Durham recalled King, on the tape of Scott Sisson's last-second field goal that upset No. 1 Virginia 41-38 in Tech's 1990 national championship season. "All you hear is 'Wooo, wooo, wooo!'" said Durham.

In May, 1999, King was diagnosed with multiple myeloma, a form of cancer. He underwent extensive treatment in Fayetteville, Ark., and recovered. But in May 2004, King was diagnosed with secondary acute myelogenous leukemia. He returned to Fayetteville for treatment, then came home with the disease in remission. But the leukemia returned in late August. After going back to Arkansas for more treatment, King came home for good in September but was unable to call Tech football games that fall.

By then, he knew that Tech was dedicating the football locker room in his name. King called it "The greatest honor of my life." He was too ill to attend the Tech-Miami game that Oct. 2. But his oldest daughter, Angela, drove her parents to Bobby Dodd Stadium just before halftime. King was helped into the back seat of the Rambling Wreck, Tech's vintage 1930 Ford.

During a halftime ceremony, he was driven around the field to thunderous applause. Then the Wreck led the Jackets back onto the field for the second half.

"He was overwhelmed [by the locker room dedication]," Durham later said. He couldn't believe that the place he loved and, in my mind, embodied, would permanently honor him that way.

"To a lot of us, Kim represents exactly what the goal is when you come here," said Durham. "You want to compete, to play, to win. But in the end you want to do it the right way and be successful—not just in football, but professionally and personally."

For me, a New York transplant-turned-longtime Atlanta sportswriter, Kim King was the quintessential Tech Man, the essence of the Institute and a pigskin soul-and-savior of football on The Flats. He was also always fine company: On the road, dining on crab cakes in Annapolis the night before a Tech-Navy game. In the car, when Al Ciraldo's exuberance occasionally, wonderfully wandered all over the radio dial. "Well actually Al..." In his candor, cooperation and the completion of this book, often during interviews in his penthouse office, even in the pain and throes of leukemia.

Thank you, Kim King. A great and courageous man.

Jack Wilkinson
Atlanta